MEET
THE AUTHORS
AND
ILLUSTRATORS

MEET
THE AUTHORS
AND
ILLUSTRATORS

60 Creators of Favorite Children's Books
Talk About Their Work

BY DEBORAH KOVACS AND JAMES PRELLER

For the authors,
who graciously granted a peek behind the scenes
DEBORAH KOVACS

For Elana and Sylvie
JAMES PRELLER

Design direction by Vincent Ceci
Book design by Jacqueline Swensen
Cover illustration by William T. Gibbons

ISBN 0-590-49097-4

24 23 22 21 20 19 18   1 2/0

Printed in the U.S.A.

Contents

Continued

Contents

INTERMEDIATE BOOKS

AUTHORS AND ILLUSTRATORS

I f books are the wings on which children's imaginations fly, then the authors and illustrators of the books are the wing-makers. It is their gifts that provide children with the magical experience derived from reading a good book. And when children learn about an author's or an illustrator's life and work, their reading often takes on new meaning.

Author/illustrator studies make books come alive. Children are challenged to make connections between a person's life and his or her work. And, in turn, children come to view their own creative work more seriously.

The sixty authors and illustrators profiled here are but a sprinkling of the thousands of people who create books for children. They were chosen because their books are perennial favorites of both children and teachers. Their books represent many styles and genres. They live in the United States, Canada, England, Japan, and New Zealand. And each has something special to say to children.

The profiles emphasize the process each person goes through in the creation of a story or illustrations. These authors and illustrators become models for children who are learning to brainstorm, draft, write, edit, rewrite, and illustrate their own stories.

This book has many uses. The profiles can serve as background for your students' individual reading as well as for small-group or class author studies. The creative activity at the end of each profile can extend the children's reading or be the spark for a new writing or drawing project. In most cases, the activity was suggested by the author specifically for this book.

But in every case, as they explore the wealth of children's literature, your students will feel the books' creators sitting beside them while they read.

PICTURE BOOKS

AUTHORS AND ILLUSTRATORS

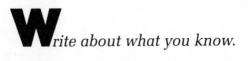 *rite about what you know.*

It's the most common advice offered to young writers. But after profiling the authors and illustrators found in the first half of this book, I'd like to make a brief addendum: *Remember, you know a lot.*

Bruce Degen may have expressed it best: "Each of us has individual things that mean something to us—things that no one else is carrying around. That's a good jumping-off point for a story. It's a place to start."

Other writers expressed the same self-affirming message in different ways. John Steptoe drew inspiration from his African heritage, Vera Williams from a canoe trip down the Yukon River, Eric Carle from the painful memory of leaving a best friend and a beloved country behind.

Each artist in this book is unique. Each draws upon personal experiences, thinks individual thoughts, and dreams solitary dreams—just like the children in our classrooms.

So when we celebrate children's authors and illustrators, we are, in fact, celebrating the potential and humanity in all of us. We celebrate every child's ability to think, to feel, to dream, and perchance—like the artists in this book—to enrich our world simply by sharing his or her world with us.

JAMES PRELLER

Mitsumasa Anno

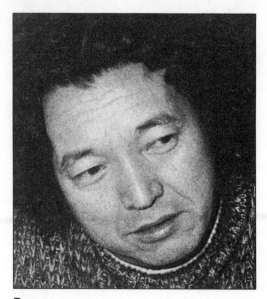

Born:
March 20, 1926, in Tsuwano, Japan

Home:
Tokyo, Japan

Mitsumasa Anno was born and raised in Tsuwano, a small mountain village in Japan. Though it was a very beautiful village surrounded by mountains, Anno yearned to learn more about the world beyond it. Anno remembers, "As a child, I always wondered what was on the other side of the mountains."

Anno's boundless curiosity pertained not only to distant lands. He was fascinated by mathematics, logic, entomology (the study of insects), and art. He also possessed a lively imagination: "I liked to observe real people and make up stories about them. If a man walked by, I would think that he must be a carpenter or a doctor on his way to see a child in the hospital or whatever."

In 1961 Anno first saw the drawings of M. C. Escher. These strange, improbable drawings excited Anno. It seemed to him that Escher's drawings were almost like puzzles, riddles from another world—the world of the imagination. Newly inspired, Anno decided to create his own, Escher-like illustrations. In the book *Topsy-Turvies: Pictures to Stretch the Imagination*, Anno created impossible pictures of ceilings that double as floors, stairways that lead *up* to a *lower* level, and water faucets that turn into rivers.

Anno wanted the book to challenge readers to see new things, think new thoughts. In a postscript to the book he explained, "I have purposely added no words to these topsy-turvy pictures of mine so you can make them mean whatever you want them to mean."

Anno soon contrived another "book without rules"—*Upside-Downers: More Pictures to Stretch the Imagination*. He said, "My pictures are like maps, which perhaps only I can understand. Therefore, in following my maps there are some travelers who get lost." But for Anno, getting lost is just one more chance to find something new.

ANNO'S JOURNEYS

Anno's first visit to Europe inspired him to write *Anno's Journey*. Anno said of his journey, "My purpose for traveling was not merely to see more of the world but to get lost in it. I did often get lost and faced many difficulties, but under such circumstances there were always unexpected discoveries and interesting experiences waiting for me."

Anno's Journey was the first of four remarkable books based on Anno's travels. The others are *Anno's Italy, Anno's Britain*, and *Anno's USA*. Perhaps the most surprising thing that Anno discovered in his travels was how similar people are to each other. He says, "Among living creatures, more things are shared than are different. Seeing a sunset in Europe, I was impressed by the natural truth that we have only one sun—that, no matter where we are, we all see the same sun."

"It seems that, although languages and customs are different in various parts of the world, there are no differences at all in our hearts."

ous George. But Anno's books rarely center on a main character. Instead, they seem to be about the world itself. Still, there is one recurring character—the lone horseman who travels through the pages of the "Journey" books. This character is the one that best represents the spirit of Anno's work— the spirit of exploration and discovery.

Anno's "Journey" books also provide readers with a treasure hunt of sorts. Hidden in the drawings are pictures of famous paintings or picture-book characters such as Goldilocks and Little Red Riding-Hood. By hiding these treasures, Anno whispers a secret into the reader's ear: The more you seek, the more you shall find.

Differences such as language, dress, and skin color are only on the surface. As Anno said, "The essence of being human is the same everywhere."

Many authors, over time, become associated with one character they created. For example, Dr. Seuss will forever be known as the man behind the Cat in the Hat, Peggy Parish is loved for her mixed-up maid named Amelia Bedelia, and H. A. Rey is famous for creating the mischievous Curi-

DO IT YOURSELF!

When he finished *Anno's Italy*, Anno said, "The book has no words, yet I feel sure that anyone who looks at it can understand what the people in the pictures are doing and what they are thinking and feeling." Do you think that's true? Try to imagine what some of the people in Anno's illustrations are thinking and feeling. Write down a conversation they might be having.

Molly Bang

SELECTED TITLES

**The Old Woman
and the Red Pumpkin**
1975

Wiley and the Hairy Man
1976

**The Old Woman
and the Rice Thief**
1978

**The Grey Lady and the
Strawberry Snatcher**
(Caldecott Honor Book)
1980

Dawn
1983

Ten, Nine, Eight
(Caldecott Honor Book)
1984

The Paper Crane
1985

Delphine
1988

Yellow Ball
1991

◆

Born:
December 29, 1943, in Princeton,
New Jersey

Home:
Woods Hole, Massachusetts

Although making a picture-book can be a long, painstaking process, Molly Bang seems to genuinely enjoy each step. Most important, Molly values the team effort that goes into making a book. She explains, "It's really a pleasure to work with editors and art directors who are trying to make this a good piece of work. At a certain point, you are working on this same thing that belongs to all of you. They want to make it better, and you want to make it better. Sometimes you just disagree on what's going to make it better."

TRY AND TRY AGAIN

Molly says, "With *The Paper Crane*, I did three versions of pictures before I did the published version. Each had a totally differ-ent style. One was Chinese brush painting; one was in pencil and white ink on gray paper, sort of like *Wiley and the Hairy Man*; the other used cut paper, but featured one character that was an old woman. The editors rejected it because they thought she looked too weird. I thought she looked wonderful."

With each rejection, Molly would shrug and say to herself, *Oh well, try again.* Finally, Molly hit upon a technique for the illus-trations that everyone loved. "I used scissors, an X-acto blade, and construction paper," Bang recalls. "I picked up the pieces with tweezers, dipped them in glue, and attached them to the paper. It took about a year to make all the pictures."

Editors helped Molly in other ways, too. Molly admits, "My ten-dency is to get too gushy and wordy. So my editors help me to revise and shorten the text." With *The Paper Crane*, her editors, Susan Hirschman and Libby Shub, suggested that the story might be improved if she included a child. Molly thought about the suggestion and agreed. She says, "I think that made it that much more interesting for me. Because then you've got two plots going on at once. The dad was just interest-ed in running a great restaurant, but the child loved the bird and lost it."

Molly points out that the boy isn't in the written story at all. "If you notice, the child is not in the words—he's just in the pictures."

In this example, you can clearly see how a story is told not only in words but also in pictures. And sometimes a picture doesn't need *any* words to tell its story. If you need proof, just take a look at Molly's wordless book, *The Grey Lady and the Strawberry Snatcher.*

Most of Molly's books are the products of endless revisions, but there are some rare exceptions. Molly recalls, "I've never had a story that just came to me out of the blue, except for *Ten, Nine, Eight*, which came to me word for word. There it was; that was the only version. I didn't make a single change. What happened was I was away from my daughter for a couple of weeks. I missed her and I wanted to write something for her. So *Ten, Nine, Eight* is what I wrote."

Molly Bang honed her writing

skills by studying folktales. As she read more and more stories from around the world, Molly began to notice recurring patterns in the stories. By imitating those patterns, Molly learned how to write stories of her own. She says, "Folktales are a beautiful, jewel-like form of writing. Emotions are never stated, but they are made clear by the actions of the characters. It's about as concise a story as a person can make."

In addition to writing and illustrating her own books, Bang spends time teaching art to children in schools. Molly believes that everyone can enjoy making art. "It's as if people think that artists and writers are these strange people who get their ideas beamed down from another planet," says Bang. "It's not as though we are different from anybody else. When I work with kids, the whole class works on projects together. Everybody contributes. Every child can write. Every child can make pictures that are special and quite wonderful."

> **"My mother can read Bengali, so she translated some folktales, which I then illustrated. There were never any problems; she was the boss of the words and I was the boss of the pictures."**

DO IT YOURSELF!

Molly Bang suggests this activity for young writers: "All stories have some kind of pattern. With the help of a teacher, identify the pattern of a story. It's easy to identify the pattern in *Ten, Nine, Eight*. The pattern for *The Paper Crane* is: man has a problem; stranger comes; man is kind to stranger; stranger solves problem. Make up your own story, following the basic pattern."

Aliki Brandenberg

SELECTED TITLES

My Five Senses
1962, revised 1989

*Corn Is Maize: The Gift
of the Indians*
1976

Mummies Made in Egypt
1979

The Two of Them
1979

Digging Up Dinosaurs
1981, revised 1988

We Are Best Friends
1982

Feelings
1984

Dinosaurs Are Different
1985

How a Book Is Made
1986

Manners
1990

Born:
September 3, 1929, in Wildwood Crest,
New Jersey

Home:
London, England

A liki (pronounced "A-leek-ee") grew up in Philadel-phia, the third of four children. "My parents were born in Greece," she says. "We spoke Greek in the house. We had Greek friends and Greek customs and ate Greek food. I was two people—I was Greek inside the house and I was American when I went to school."

When Aliki was in kinder-garten, her teacher told her parents, "Your daughter will be an artist one day." Aliki remembers, "I was always drawing, all through my life. I was just lucky to have a teacher who recognized my talent. When you are young it's called talent, later on it becomes hard work and perseverance."

The subjects of Aliki's books range from dinosaurs to mum-mies, from medieval feasts to friendship and feelings. She even wrote a book about making books. Aliki says, "My writing takes two distinct directions. I write fiction, which comes from within, and nonfiction 'research books' about subjects that I want to learn more about.

"Writing and illustrating books," she says, "is a way of sat-isfying my curiosity. I'm just lucky that children are curious about the same things I am."

But where does Aliki find all those ideas? "Everything that I write comes from inside of me. My nonfiction books come from an interest in something, like the book *Mummies Made in Egypt*," she says. "I had never seen mum-mified animals before I visited the British Museum. I became so interested I thought I'd write a book about the wrapping process. I read and read and read, did all my research, and found out every-thing except why mummies are wrapped in those patterns. That's the way it happens sometimes."

The way Aliki describes it, book ideas slowly take shape in the back of her mind, like bread dough rising. Suddenly, an experi-ence or remark will trigger an idea. She explains, "When we moved to London from New York, I missed my family and friends. Then a friend remarked that her little boy drew pictures to send to his friend who had moved away. That inspired the book *We Are Best Friends*."

Another book, *The Two of Them*, is her most personal. "I wrote it when my father died. The child in the story is a cross between my daughter Alexa and myself. It's really told through her eyes. The ring in the book, for instance, is the ring that my father made when she was born. I wrote that book just to get my feelings out."

BACK TO THE DRAWING BOARD

Once Aliki has an idea, the hard work really begins. "I work at least twelve hours a day," she admits. "I can sit for eight hours at my desk without even *thinking* about food. And I can stay in my house for eight days without going out!"

For Aliki, the words come before the pictures. "Even though I have visual images while I am

> **"I call my work hard fun. It's something I love and need to do, like breathing. I love the challenge that each day brings—the hard part as much as the fun part."**

writing, they very often don't turn out the way I thought." Sometimes the words come easily. But other times, it's a struggle. Here's how Aliki solves writer's block:

DO IT YOURSELF!

If you hope to become an artist, you can practice by drawing pictures of your toes. Aliki did. "I used to draw my toes all the time. And my feet. They were very hard to draw. I couldn't draw my hands as easily, because I was using them. So I drew my feet."

"If I can't get a story the way I want it, I put it aside for a time and do something else. Then I go back and see it with new eyes."

Sometimes, Aliki will share her problems with an editor. "My editor at Greenwillow, Susan Hirschman, helped me very much with the book *Feelings*. I wrote it, but when it came time to do the illustrations I didn't know how to do it. I said to her, 'I don't think

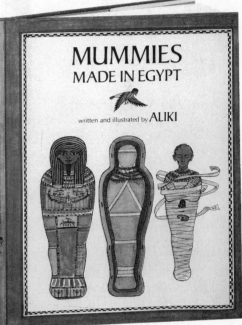

you want this book anymore because I don't know how to illustrate it.' But she said, 'You don't have to make *big* pictures—you can make *little* pictures.' That one comment helped me so much."

Aliki has also illustrated a number of books written by her husband, Franz Brandenberg. When she's not writing or illustrating books, Aliki loves gardening, films, traveling, baking, and reading. But Aliki is so busy, she admits that she doesn't find time to read as much as she would like. So, she says, "I go to the mountains, take a stack of books, and read for my vacation."

Ashley Bryan

SELECTED TITLES

*The Ox of the
Wonderful Horns and
Other African Folktales*
1971

*Walk Together Children:
Black American Spirituals*
1974

The Dancing Granny
1977

*Beat the Story-Drum,
Pum-Pum*
1980

The Cat's Purr
1985

*Lion and the
Ostrich Chicks and Other
African Folktales*
1986

*All Night, All Day:
A Child's First Book of
African-American
Spirituals*
1991

◆

Born:
July 13, 1923, in New York, New York

Home:
Islesford, Maine

Remembering his many visits to schools, Ashley Bryan says, "Kids often ask if I've won awards. I say, yes, I have won awards. But I also talk about when I did my first ABC book in kindergarten. My mamma hugged and kissed me. My father spun me around. My sisters and brothers said, 'Hooray, Ashley!' My teacher said, 'You are the author, the illustrator, the binder. And when you take it home, you are the distributor too!' When I told her about the reception I got at home, she said, 'Well, you are getting rave reviews for that book of yours. So let's keep on publishing books!'

"That reaction," Ashley warmly recalls, "is still the greatest award I've ever received—the response of family, friends, neighbors, and teachers. It's an award children can experience them-selves. I tell kids, 'Now is the time of great awards.'"

Ashley Bryan is a treasure hunter. He seeks treasures from the ancient days of Africa and brings them back for modern-day children to enjoy. But his treasures aren't gold coins or rare jewels. They are the folk stories the African people once told.

"Stories are always a treasury of the history of a people," Ashley says. "African tales are a beautiful means of linking the living Africa, past and present, to our own present. What the African sees in his world, the questions he asks, and the things that he feels and imagines have all found their way into the stories."

Spending long hours in libraries, Ashley Bryan searches in scholarly books for African folktales. He then retells those stories in his own words, hoping to bring them alive for a new genera-

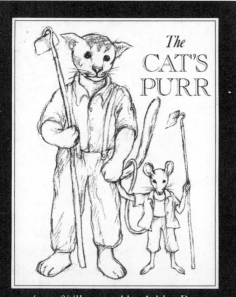

written & illustrated by Ashley Bryan

tion of readers.

Ashley explains, "When I write, I'm trying to find the *sound* of the voice in the printed word. That's what I'm always after. I'm usually working from forms that simply document the basic story. They may be just a few sentences or just a paragraph or two. They were not intended to convey anything of what it is when you tell a story. I look at those words and say, 'Nobody would tell a story like that!' "

Ashley's job, as he sees it, is to recapture the spirit of the original stories. He says, "I want to get across the feeling of the storyteller so that the person reading it will feel the presence of the story-teller." In this way, Ashley's written stories capture the mood of the period in which the stories were first told—a time when a circle of people gathered around the storyteller.

WRITING WITH THE EAR

According to Ashley, the *ear* is an important element of a story. That's because he works within the storytelling tradition, where there is always a voice to speak the words and an ear to hear them. The sound of spoken words, he believes, is like a song. And he always tries to make that song as beautiful as possible.

Ashley says, "My first version states the basic story. I will then try speaking it, hearing it. Then I'll go on to a second version, a third, a fourth. At each stage, I will test it with my voice. Then I'll go back to the writing. By the time I reach a fifth version, it begins to have its own voice. Finally, the story reaches the point where I can say to it, 'You are alive!'"

"I hope that my work with the African tales will be, by the very nature of storytelling, like a tender bridge reaching us across distances of time and space."

LION and the Ostrich Chicks

Retold and illustrated by ASHLEY BRYAN

If Ashley Bryan seems particularly fond of the sound of words, it might be because he inherited a love of music from his parents.

"One of my earliest recollections is of my mother singing. She sang from one end of the day to the other. My father used to say, 'Son, your mother must think she's a bird.' My father loved birds. The living rooms of our various Bronx apartments were always lined with shelves, not for books but for birds. Once I counted over a hundred birds in his collection. My mother used to say, 'If I want any attention around here, I'll have to get in a cage.' "

Eric Carle

Born:
June 25, 1929, in Syracuse, New York

Home:
Northampton, Massachusetts

Out of all the questions kids ask Eric Carle, "Where do ideas come from?" is the one he hears most often. Although Eric thinks it would take hours to fully respond, he offers this answer: "Of course, the question of where ideas come from is the most difficult of all. Some people like to say they get ideas when they're in the shower. That's always a very entertaining answer, but I think it's much deeper than that. It goes back to your upbringing, your education, and so forth." To Eric, ideas don't come from one place. They come from all the experiences in his life, all the thoughts in his mind, and all the feelings in his heart.

A BRIDGE TO AMERICA

Eric Carle was born in Syracuse, New York, to German immigrants. When Eric was six, he and his parents moved back to Germany. Eric hated the strict discipline of his new German school. Sad and confused, Eric longed to return to America. "When it became apparent that we would not return, I decided that I would become a bridge builder. I would build a bridge from Germany to America and take my beloved German grandmother by the hand across the wide ocean."

It would be seventeen years before Eric returned. In a sense, this difficult period was a great source of inspiration for Eric's later books. As an artist, Eric strives to help children enjoy school more than he did. He says, "I am fascinated by the period in a child's life when he or she, for the first time, leaves home to go to school. I should like my books to bridge that great divide."

Growing up, Eric loved to walk through the woods with his father. He fondly recalls, "He'd turn over a

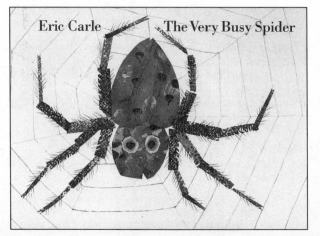

Eric Carle   The Very Busy Spider

rock and show me the little creatures that scurried and slithered about." On these walks, filled with stories and discovery, Eric learned to love nature. Giving us another clue to where he finds his ideas, Eric says, "I try to recall that feeling when I write my books."

Sometimes ideas for Eric's books came from just fooling around. At least that's how he describes the inception of *The Very Hungry Caterpillar*. "I playfully punched a hole into a stack of papers. I thought, A bookworm at work! Not enough for a book, but, nevertheless, a beginning."

Eventually, Eric submitted his story about the bookworm, who had been changed to a green worm named Willy. His editor liked the idea—almost. She asked, "How about a caterpillar?" And so Eric Carle's most famous book was born.

By the way, Eric already knows that a caterpillar emerges from a chrysalis, not a cocoon! So don't bother writing to tell him. Eric explains how the famous "mistake" crept into the book:

"My editor contacted a scientist, who said that it was permissible to use the word *cocoon*. Poetry over science. It simply would not have worked to say, 'Come out of your chrysalis!' If we can accept giants tied down by dwarfs, genies in bottles, and knights who attack windmills, why can't a caterpillar come out of a cocoon?"

The most important part of developing a book, Eric believes, is working with editors to revise it. He says, "You have doubts. You hate it. You love it. You discuss it with your editors. You change it. Finally, at one point you just know it's right. After that it goes

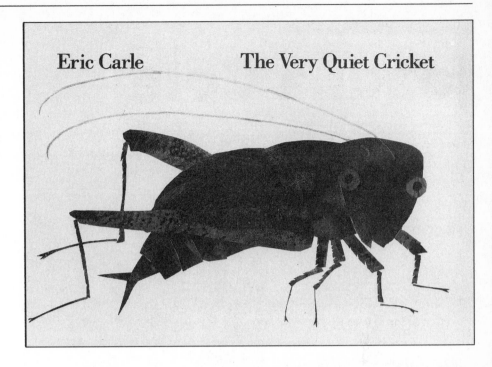

"I want children to know that learning can be fun, delightful, interesting, silly."

◆

very quickly. The art for *The Tiny Seed* took only two weeks!"

And so, where *do* ideas come from? Eric likes the answer that his Uncle August used to give. "I'd say, 'Uncle August, tell me a story.' Peering over his glasses he'd say, 'First you have to wind up my thinking machine.' And, as I had done many times before, I began to wind an imaginary lever near his temple. After a little while—all along he had made whirring noises—he shouted, 'Halt! I have a story for you!' "

Eric says, "I like my Uncle August's answer to where stories come from. They come from your thinking machine. All you have to do is wind it up."

DO IT YOURSELF!

Team up with a friend to write and illustrate your own version of *The Very Hungry Caterpillar*. Follow the original pattern of the book but make a few key changes. (The Very Hungry Monster? The Very Sleepy Puppy? The Very, Very Weird Kid?)

Joanna Cole

SELECTED TITLES

A Frog's Body
1980

Cars and How They Go
1983

Bony-Legs
1983

How You Were Born
1984

The Magic School Bus At the Water Works
1986

The Magic School Bus Inside the Earth
1987

Evolution
1987

The Magic School Bus Lost in the Solar System
1990

My Puppy Is Born
1991

◆

Born:
August 11, 1944, in Newark, New Jersey

Home:
Sandy Hook, Connecticut

What's Joanna Cole interested in? Well, just about *everything*. And when Joanna Cole is interested in something, she usually writes a book about it. She's written about fleas, cockroaches, dinosaurs, chicks, fish, saber-toothed tigers, frogs, horses, snakes, cars, puppies, insects, and (whew!) babies.

"I was never one of those wonderful students who gets straight A's and everything right on the tests," says Joanna Cole. "But I've always been obsessed with logical thinking. I used to argue with my teachers when things didn't make sense to me."

Joanna grew up in East Orange, New Jersey. Her interest in science grew from her natural curiosity about the world in which she lived. "We had a small backyard, and I was the gardener in the family. I spent a lot of time planting flowers, daydreaming, watching ants, and catching bugs."

IT BEGAN WITH COCKROACHES

All writers must begin somewhere, and Joanna Cole began her career by writing about cockroaches. Joanna was working as a library-teacher in a Brooklyn elementary school when her father gave her an article. Joanna remembers, "It was about cockroaches and how they were here before the dinosaurs. It got me thinking about all those science books I'd read as a kid—insects had been a special interest of mine—and it occurred to me that there wasn't one about cockroaches."

As a nonfiction writer, Joanna does a lot of research before she writes a single word. "The impossible dream is to know everything," she says. "When you are writing the book, you must select what you want to go into the book. What always happens is that more things are left out than can go in.

"I have a question that I ask myself as I write: Why does the reader want to turn the page? I never feel that kids are going to turn the page just because it's there to turn. There has to be a question that's in a reader's mind—and he or she turns the page to find the answers.

"Kids often ask me if it's fun to be a writer. That question always leaves me a little speechless.

Because the answer is, of course, yes and no. When it's going well, there's nothing more exhilarating. But it's so much work!"

Joanna has been praised by both teachers and children for being able to make science interesting and understandable. And now, with the *Magic School Bus* series, she's done the impossible—she's made science funny.

"Before I started writing the first *Magic School Bus* book, I had a lot of lofty goals—and I had no idea whether they could be achieved. I wanted it to be a very good science book. I also wanted it to be a good story, a story you might read even without the science. And I wanted it to be genuinely funny. Well, this was terrifying to me. I couldn't work at all. I cleaned out closets, answered letters, went shopping—anything but sit down and write. But eventually I did it, even though I was scared."

The *Magic School Bus* books were a huge success. Readers across the country loved them. They especially loved the wacky science teacher, Ms. Frizzle. "We were concerned that teachers might be offended by Ms. Frizzle, with her crazy clothes. But what's happened is that teachers love her. Whenever Bruce Degen, the illustrator, and I go to schools, there's almost always somebody dressed as Ms. Frizzle. The teachers are even asking for Ms. Frizzle outfits."

In addition to her many science books, Joanna Cole has written over twenty books of fiction including *Don't Tell the Whole World*, *The Clown-Arounds*, *Bony-Legs*, *Doctor Change*, *Monster Manners*, and *The Missing Tooth*.

Joanna Cole finds pleasure and

"When I'm writing a book, it's almost as if I'm building a cabinet. I want it all to fit together. I work very hard at that."

excitement in each new project she takes on. "When I was starting to write *The Magic School Bus Inside the Human Body*, I didn't know whose body the bus would travel in. Then I thought of the idea that Ms. Frizzle and her class would go into Arnold's body, and that he would eat them as Cheesie Wheesies. That was one of the happiest moments of my life. I was walking on clouds all day."

DO IT YOURSELF!

Joanna Cole says kids sometimes write their own *Magic School Bus* adventures. Here's her advice: "Start by picking a topic and a place for the field trip. Do a lot of research. Think of a story line—and come up with lots of jokes. Some kids like to put their own teacher and class into the story."

Donald Crews

SELECTED TITLES

Freight Train
(Caldecott Honor Book)
1978

Truck
(Caldecott Honor Book)
1980

Light
1981

Carousel
1982

Parade
1983

School Bus
1984

Bicycle Race
1985

Flying
1986

◆

Born:
August 30, 1938, in Newark,
New Jersey

Home:
Brooklyn, New York

Donald Crews collects ideas. One of his favorite activities is to wander around the city looking for images that excite and interest him. "I do it all the time," Crews says. "I don't think I'm ever without a camera and a sketchbook. I use both of them for collecting ideas."

At this point, camera in hand, Crews isn't thinking about making a book. Instead, he's seeking a beginning—an inspiration, an idea that may lead to another idea. "My images, or my ideas, are reality-based. They all start someplace—most likely with a photograph."

The subjects for his books are always drawn from real life. It may be a city parade, the memory of a childhood train journey, a carousel in an amusement park, or the flight of an airplane. His books remind us that everyday life is interesting and exciting. All you have to do is look closely.

Truck was inspired by living in the city near a commercial truck depot. Crews, always on the lookout for something visually exciting, became fascinated with the trucks. Crews remembers, "Each day trucks delivered and picked up all kinds of goods and performed all sorts of services. A lot of these trucks were red, and all had great typographic images on their sides."

DEVELOPING IDEAS

How does Crews develop an idea into a book? The process goes something like this: "Once I become fascinated with a subject, I'll do some freewheeling sketches. At that point, I'm not really putting a book together, I'm just thinking it through and exploring

24

the visual possibilities."

The next step is to create tiny thumbnail sketches. Crews says, "This way I can see, roughly, all thirty-two pages of the book. I'll know the sequence of events before I start to illustrate."

Words come next. But for Donald Crews, the central focus is always on the pictures. "I'm not primarily a writer, and I think the pictures are more effective than the words," Crews states. "I'm continually paring down the number of words I'm using. I'm also trimming down and tightening up the illustrations to make them more effective.

"I really believe in the idea of a *picture*-book. A picture-book is a book that really ought to tell the story with pictures. If it takes too many words to make it work, then it isn't a picture book anymore." With this in mind, Crews returns again and again to his text, revising and eliminating words.

The plot, or action of the book, may be surprisingly simple. A truck picks up a load and travels to its destination. A carousel takes on riders, revolves, and stops. By focusing on a simple action, Crews seeks to capture the excitement of the action. Sometimes he'll go to great lengths to achieve the effect of motion.

The book *Carousel* features some exciting pages, which show all sorts of blurred movement. "It's actually photography," Crews explains. "The primary illustration is a drawn-and-painted carousel. Then I took a series of color photographs of that piece of art, moving the camera to create the illusion of movement.

"I used that same idea, without a camera, for *Freight Train*. But in order to get the same kind of

"I took pictures of bicycle races for years, never thinking they'd be the subject of a book. But, eventually, those photos lead to *Bicycle Race.*"

motion in a carousel—which is much more complicated in terms of drawing—I thought that photography would be a good way to do it." After many experiments (and several rolls of film) Crews finally had the effect he wanted.

Readers can look forward to many more books from Donald Crews. And with each one, it seems, comes a journey—on a plane, in a parade, on a freight train. But no matter where the journey leads, everyone is invited. All you have to do is pick up a book, bring your imagination, and climb aboard!

DO IT YOURSELF!

You can have a lot of fun making your own book based on the themes in Donald Crews's books. Take *Light*, for example. Draw your own pictures of lights, using familiar objects from your everyday life. Or create your own themes—circles, cars, or whatever interests you.

Bruce Degen

SELECTED TITLES

◆

Born:
June 14, 1945, in Brooklyn, New York

Home:
Newtown, Connecticut

Fantasy plays an important role in Bruce Degen's books. But each story or illustration, Bruce says, begins with a close look at everyday life.

Bruce explains, "Even though my style is not strictly realistic, the shapes that I put into my drawings come from looking at real things. For instance, when I created Commander Toad, I first did pages and pages of research sketches on toads and frogs."

When creating a character, Bruce usually begins by making realistic drawings. Gradually, after completing many sketches, he'll add lots of personality to those realistic drawings. For Bruce Degen, the process clearly works; he's helped bring to life many memorable children's book characters: Commander Toad, Jesse Bear, the Forgetfuls, and, of course, Ms. Frizzle.

What's the most difficult thing about inventing a new character? Bruce admits, "The hardest thing to do is make it turn around—to draw it from the front and the side and still make it look like the same character." With a modest laugh, Bruce confesses, "I don't always do that so well!"

CATCHING IDEAS

As a helpful reference, Bruce keeps files of pictures that he's clipped from magazines. That way, if he needs to see a picture of a rabbit, he simply turns to the file. For a recent project, Bruce had to draw a mouse. Bruce says, "I didn't have too many good pictures of mice in my files." Always creative, Bruce found a clever solution—in his basement!

He explains, "As it turns out, we had mice in the basement, so I went out and got a live trap. I

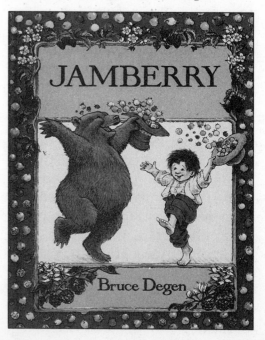

caught a whole family of mice and I've got them in a cage in the basement. Rather than have them running around chewing up things, we decided to have them as guests for the winter. We feed them, we talk to them, and I draw them. So I solved two problems at once!"

Bruce has written only four of the books he has illustrated, but he hopes to write more in the future. The problem is, he gets so much work as an illustrator there just aren't enough hours in the day to write! "I'm a very slow writer and a very fast illustrator," Bruce says. "Whenever I'm given a manuscript that's fun, I do that and forget about writing for a little while."

The best-loved of the books Bruce has authored is undoubtedly the whimsical *Jamberry*. Even this fantasy story, Bruce claims, has its foundations in real life. "*Jamberry* grew out of personal experience. You see, I grew up in a very urban part of the city. There was no grass or gardens, just sidewalks and cement. In the summer, we used to go up to the Catskill Mountains, and it was totally the opposite. The world was generous. The berries were free, like a gift. When I wanted to do a book about being young and joyful, I remembered those berry-picking trips. I made up a nonsense rhyme using the names of berries. The point is, I started by pulling something out of my memory that meant something to me."

Bruce finds that by illustrating a book, he usually discovers new things about the story. "When I started *Jamberry*, I thought I was the little boy in the story. But halfway through the book, while I was doing the drawing of the boy and bear going over the waterfall

in the canoe, I suddenly understood that I was the bear and the little boy was my son."

A lifelong New Yorker, Bruce recently moved to a new home in Connecticut. "When I lived in the city," Bruce says, "I used to get on the subway and ride to my studio, stay there all day, and then come home. But now I work at home. In the morning I pick up my cup of coffee and say to my wife, 'I'm off to the office, dear!' and walk upstairs. It sure beats the subway."

> "Each of us has individual things that mean something to us, things that no one else is carrying around. That's a good jumping off point for a story. It's a place to start."

DO IT YOURSELF!

In *Jamberry*, Bruce made up a nonsense poem about his favorite food—berries. Read *Jamberry* and then write your own silly poem. It could be about pizza, hamburgers, ice cream, or anything you like.

Tomie dePaola

SELECTED TITLES

The Cloud Book:
Words and Pictures
1975

Strega Nona: An Old Tale
(Caldecott Honor Book)
1975

The Quicksand Book
1977

The Popcorn Book
1978

Francis, the Poor Man
of Assisi
1982

The Legend of the
Bluebonnet: An Old Tale
of Texas
1983

Tomie dePaola's
Mother Goose
1984

The Art Lesson
1989

◆

Born:
September 15, 1934, in Meriden,
Connecticut

Home:
New London, New Hampshire

With more than 170 books to his credit, Tomie dePaola (pronounced "de-POW-la") knows something about ideas. In fact, he's bursting with them. When he's working on one book, he's usually thinking about the next book. He's never had writer's block, though he does confess to a single, brief bout with "artist's block." For Tomie, the ideas keep flowing, book after book after book.

Tomie dePaola believes that many people give up on their ideas too easily. He says, "I think if you have an idea, you should hang on to it. Write it down and think about it for a while. Sometimes nothing happens with ideas. But some of them eventually become books."

The important thing about ideas, the prolific dePaola believes, is to explore them. "Ideas are like doors," dePaola says. "It might just be a door that gets you to another door. But it might lead you to the secret door that opens up to the green meadow outside the castle."

According to dePaola, "We're not encouraged to take an idea that comes into our head and explore it to see if it's good or not. When a kid gets an idea that doesn't seem to fit into his teacher's or his parents' mode, they say, 'That's not a good idea.' An example is when my brother and I would have the idea of going to the amusement park. We would say, 'Can we go to the park?' My mother would respond, 'That's not a good idea.'

"But we, of course, thought it was a terrific idea. Instead of giving up on it, my brother and I would join forces. Suddenly we'd do the dishes, help around house, and start dropping little hints. Eventually our parents would give in and we'd be taken to the amusement park. The whole process might take two or three weeks. The point is, we would work on the idea. We'd develop it. We'd say, 'Let's not give up this idea.' "

FEEDING THE IMAGINATION

Although Tomie dePaola's books include nonfiction and fiction, he generally draws upon his childhood as a source for inspiration and guidance. An example can be found in his book *The Art Lesson*.

Tomie recalls, "*The Art Lesson* is based on something that actually happened. I never forgot that incident. I had been telling that story for years when my editor, Margaret Frith, suggested that it might make a good book. So I sat down and wrote the same story I had been telling."

To create his artwork, dePaola needs to be in his studio, surrounded by his beloved materials. "But," dePaola adds with a laugh, "that's not true for writing. I can write anywhere! I have written drafts of manuscripts on airplanes. It's easy. You just put on your walkman, flip down the table, and write."

Tomie explains, "I do a first draft that no one sees but me. I do a lot of my writing in my head first, just thinking the story through. Usually, it's a revised second draft that gets typed neatly and sent along to my editor. Then my editor reads it and makes suggestions. We often work on the final draft together. We sit down, side by side, and write together."

Tomie dePaola has had a lifelong interest in folktales. The tales

"I think going to the movies or taking a walk or cooking pizza, is fun. Sitting down and doing books is not fun. It's my job. I take my job as seriously as I would if I were a brain surgeon."

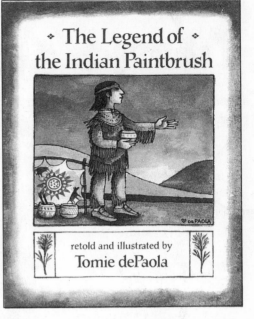

may be Italian, Irish, African, or Native American in origin—it doesn't matter to dePaola. According to him, all stories offer some insight into ourselves. He says, "I'm very into celebrating the differences between people. In celebrating ethnic differences we often discover how much people are really the same. People are people. They all have feelings. Ultimately, native customs are all focused on the same thing—to help us learn about life."

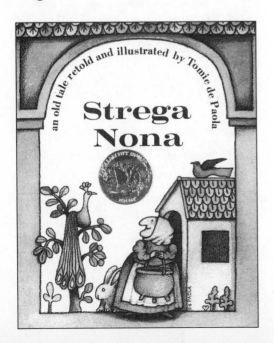

DO IT YOURSELF!

Before he wrote about it, Tomie dePaola used to talk about the event that inspired his book *The Art Lesson*. Think of a real-life story that you would like to tell your friends. Instead of talking about it, write it down. After all, everybody has stories— but it's a writer who takes the time to put them on paper.

Diane and Leo Dillon

SELECTED TITLES

The Ring in the Prairie:
A Shawnee Legend
1970

The Untold Tale
1971

The Hundred Penny Box
1975

Why Mosquitoes
Buzz in People's Ears: A
West African Tale
(Caldecott Medal)
1975

Ashanti to Zulu: African
Traditions
(Caldecott Medal)
1976

Who's in Rabbit's House:
A Masai Tale
1977

The People Could Fly:
American Black Folktales
1985

The Porcelain Cat
1987

The Tale of the
Mandarin Ducks
1990

Diane Dillon, Born:
March 13, 1933, in Glendale, California

Leo Dillon, Born:
March 2, 1933, in Brooklyn, New York

Home:
Brooklyn, New York

Are two heads better than one? Well, if the heads are Leo and Diane Dillon's, the answer is a resounding "Yes!"

Both Leo and Diane are gifted artists. But, as Leo says, "Together we are able to create art we would not be able to do individually."

Leo explains the process this way: "Each illustration is passed back and forth between us several times before it is completed, and since we both work on every piece of art, the finished painting looks as if one artist has done it."

Diane agrees, "When we sit down and start throwing ideas back and forth, one inspires the other and triggers new thoughts, new directions. That process brings about a type of thinking Leo and I could not achieve if we were working separately."

Sharing and cooperation were not always the case for Leo and Diane. When they first met as art students in New York City, they were both impressed by the other's work, but each also felt somewhat threatened by the other's talent.

"It wasn't merely a matter of competition," Leo recalls, "it was war. We spent a lot of time and energy trying to prove ourselves to each other. In the midst of all that we fell in love."

After their marriage, Leo and Diane decided to work as an illustrating team. Diane explains, "The competition between us was still so strong that we knew we would never survive separate careers. We felt that working as a team would probably help keep our marriage together."

Leo believes that the key to their success was developing a technique that allows them to share the creative process. "It is important," he says, "that we work on the same piece of art in such a way that nobody knows who did what.

"After years and years of collaboration we have reached a point where our work is done by an agent we call the third artist." The mysterious third artist, according to Leo and Diane, is a combination of their talents, feelings, and ideas.

Working together isn't always easy. Occasionally there are small arguments. "Sometimes we do disagree," Diane admits. "We argue over things and get mad at each other, but that's life!"

After years of sharing the same studio, Diane and Leo now work in separate studios in their brownstone home. Leo confesses that sharing a studio was sometimes difficult. "I tend to like to play the music loud, and Diane doesn't like that. I also have a habit of playing a song, if I like it, about forty times in a row. I just keep playing it over and over. It's wonderful!" Laughing, Diane chimes in, "It can drive you crazy too."

A WEALTH OF POSSIBILITY

After Leo and Diane read a manuscript and decide they want to illustrate it, they select which style and technique will work best for the book. One day, a particularly strong manuscript arrived at their home, Verna Aardema's *Why Mosquitoes Buzz in People's Ears.* "When we first read the manuscript," Diane recalls, "we were both amazed that in just a few pages there was such a wealth of material. We were both quite delighted with all the visual possibilities."

This splendid story brought forth some of the Dillons's most original work. Diane said, "Our real feeling about aiming for perfection began with *Mosquitoes.* Suddenly it seemed that neither of us could tolerate even a tiny flaw, a minute speck on the black night

Why Mosquitoes Buzz in People's Ears
Verna Aardema | pictures by
Leo and Diane Dillon

sky, and we strove for artistic perfection on that book more than on any other before it."

The Dillons do much more than illustrate words. Through their art, they enrich the story by adding small touches, new layers of meaning. In 1976 they were awarded the Caldecott Medal for *Mosquitoes.* Diane recalled, "In a way, when *Mosquitoes* won the Caldecott Medal, it was as much a reward for us as an award. We had worked harder to achieve perfection—although, of course, we didn't achieve it—than we ever had before, and people somehow knew it."

> "It was years and years before we could pass a piece of work back and forth between us and not get into a fight."

DO IT YOURSELF

The Dillons work as a team. As a result, their illustrations have a richness and beauty that could not be achieved if the two artists worked independently. To appreciate their creative process, try working on an art project with a partner. Like Leo and Diane, you'll have to discuss the project before deciding which materials to use. You'll also have to learn how to trust and respect each other's abilities.

Phoebe Gilman

SELECTED TITLES

The Balloon Tree
1984

Jillian Jiggs
1988

**The Wonderful Pigs of
Jillian Jiggs**
1989

Grandma and the Pirates
1990

◆

Born:
April 4, 1940, in New York, New York

Home:
Toronto, Ontario, Canada

Phoebe Gilman doesn't get ideas—the ideas get her. Phoebe says, "You get obsessed with this kernel of an idea, and no matter how hard you try to ignore it, it keeps working away at you."

That initial idea may be a passing comment she overhears, something funny she sees, or a thought that floats through her mind. But once the idea grabs hold, there's no letting go. "Some of my books are very easy to write," Phoebe says. "Others just go on and on until I think, Oh, am I ever going to do anything with this idea or is it going to torture me forever?"

The Balloon Tree serves as a good example. Phoebe says that she had the basic idea for more than ten years. But ideas alone are not books. "The idea is just the beginning," Phoebe explains.

"What's important is the determination to sit down and work at it. Without an idea, you're nowhere."

Phoebe admits there are times when the ideas simply don't come. She says, "I've learned that there are times when I just have to run away from my ideas. I often think of the 'Sesame Street' character who composes songs on the piano. Instead of 'Mary had a little lamb' he'll sing, '*Mary had a little dog.*' Then he gets frustrated, bangs his head on the piano, and cries, 'I'll never get it right.' I identify with that feeling completely."

Though she tries to avoid it, Phoebe does bang her head on the piano a few times before she's satisfied with a book. "It's like with *Grandma and the Pirates*," Phoebe recalls. "The story started out as 'Grandma's Chocolate Chicken.' It went through *so many* drafts. But I've learned to tell myself, Okay, calm down. I guess you're just going to have to go shopping." But, she gleefully adds, "It can get expensive."

Written and Illustrated by Phoebe Gilman

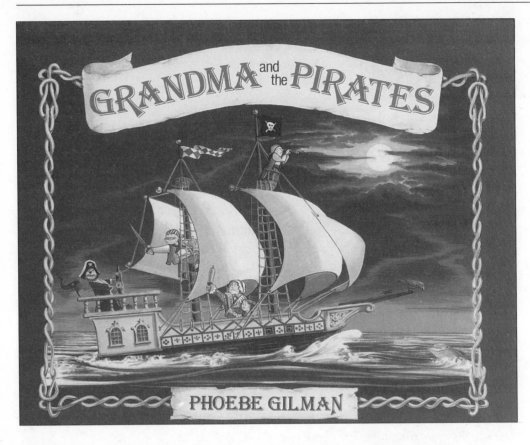

GRANDMA and the PIRATES

PHOEBE GILMAN

At the beginning of the writing process, Phoebe—who both writes and illustrates her books—will write down whatever pops into her head, without worrying whether it's good. Phoebe describes the process: "I write very freely at first, just tons of stuff. At that stage, I try not to revise at all. If the editor in my head comes in too soon and says, Ugh, this isn't good, then nothing ever gets past the early stages."

A THOUSAND AND ONE HATS

Afterwards, when Phoebe reads it back, she switches from writer to editor. She deletes words, crosses out paragraphs, throws entire pages away. Finally, when Phoebe Gilman the editor is satisfied, Phoebe Gilman the illustrator steps in.

Phoebe confesses, "I must have a thousand and one hats like Dr. Seuss's Bartholomew Cubbins.

Because when my editor's hat comes off, I have to put on my illustrator's hat. I have to look at the story and say to myself, Arrgh, how am I going to draw this? I don't know how to draw horses, I grew up in the Bronx."

Phoebe often likes to use models for her pictures. Using models, she believes, helps keep her illustrations from getting stale. "I think if you draw only from your head, then all of your characters begin to look alike. But when you go back to drawing real people, you start to notice things. You say, Oh, my goodness, look at the weird shape of his ears."

When the book is finally completed, Phoebe sends it off to the publisher. For her, this creates a feeling of emptiness, as if a good friend just moved away. Phoebe recalls, "You say to yourself, What am I going to play with now?"

And so the process begins once again.

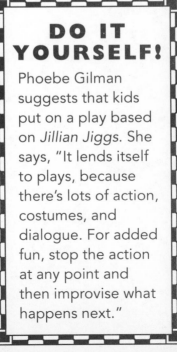

DO IT YOURSELF!

Phoebe Gilman suggests that kids put on a play based on *Jillian Jiggs*. She says, "It lends itself to plays, because there's lots of action, costumes, and dialogue. For added fun, stop the action at any point and then improvise what happens next."

Pat Hutchins

SELECTED TITLES

Rosie's Walk
1968

The Wind Blew
1974

Follow That Bus!
1977

Happy Birthday, Sam
1978

1 Hunter
1982

**You'll Soon Grow Into
Them, Titch**
1983

The Very Worst Monster
1985

The Doorbell Rang
1986

◆

Born:
June 18, 1942, in Yorkshire, England

Home:
London, England

Pat Hutchins's very first book, *Rosie's Walk*, is a widely loved classic. But without the help of a great editor, the book might never have been published.

Rosie's Walk, a story that uses only thirty-two words, was once quite different from its final version. "It started off much longer," Pat recalls. "I wrote this extremely boring story that went on forever about animal noises. I remember my editor, Susan Hirschman, reading it. There was one line that said, *This is the fox. He never makes a noise.* Out of all my reams and reams of pages, she said, 'I like that line.' "

With that advice, Pat Hutchins returned to her home, determined to revise the manuscript. Pat says, "I took her quite literally: *The fox doesn't make a noise.* So I began

to look at the book as if it were a silent film. The audience is aware of what's going on, but the heroine, Rosie, is totally unaware. I think that makes it more exciting, because the reader is in on the joke from the very beginning. The reader has secret knowledge.

"I deliberately designed the book so that the reader, turning the page, is responsible for all the fox's terrible mishaps. I like to think that readers feel very involved in the book: Their action of turning the page creates the action of the story."

OLD SNEAKERS AND PICTURES

The sixth of seven children, Pat grew up in Yorkshire, England. As a child, she often copied pictures from magazines. Pat has a fond memory of an elderly couple, Mr. and Mrs. Bruce, who encouraged her talent. "If I did a particularly good drawing," Pat recalls, "they would reward me with a bar of chocolate."

When Pat completes a book, she says, "It's always with a big sigh of relief. I love the writing, but I do find drawing very, very difficult. I'm usually amazed that I've actually managed to finish the drawings." Soon another feeling creeps in: self-doubt. "Each time I finish a book, I think, That's it, I'll never ever have another idea again! I get quite desperate."

Pat gets ideas from a variety of sources, mostly from observing her own children or remembering feelings from her own childhood.

Pat says, "There's no magic formula for coming up with ideas. You've got to try to write about what you know or what you care about. Because generally, if you enjoy something, then there's a good chance that the person reading it will enjoy it as well."

Pat begins each book the same way. "I always start with the words," she says. "I think of myself as a writer first. You can have a beautifully illustrated book, but if it has a terrible story then you can't get away with it."

Pat works in a tiny studio in her London home. She admits, "It's extremely untidy, very messy. It's full of odd things, because I need lots of things for reference.

There could be anything in here: old boots, broken old toys, all sorts of junk."

Why all the junk? Pat offers this explanation: "I'm not very good, for example, at drawing shoes. I don't think I can draw a shoe from memory, so I have a pair of old sneakers in my workroom, just so I can have a look at them, to remind myself what sneakers look like."

Pat confides that her two sons often sneak into her studio to 'borrow' paints and pencils. Laughing, she complains, "I have a sign on the door that says 'Pat's Room,' but they keep ignoring it!"

Writing books for children keeps Pat Hutchins on her toes. Though she is always very careful with research, mistakes can happen. And when one does, a smart reader will point it out to her.

Pat recalls one such incident: "The whole crux of *The Mona-Lisa Mystery* is that the *Mona Lisa* is stolen, wrapped around someone's leg, and then covered in a bandage—that's how they escape from the museum with it. One day a child wrote to me and said, 'I enjoyed your book very much, but there's one enormous mistake in it. The *Mona Lisa* is painted on wood, no way could it be wrapped around someone's leg!' So I checked with an art historian, and sure enough, it's painted on wood. It served me right!"

> "I think if I drew from now until doomsday, I would never be completely happy with my drawings."

DO IT YOURSELF!

In creating a story, a writer is often a problem-solver. For example, in *The Mona-Lisa Mystery*, Pat Hutchins had to figure out a way to steal the painting. Unfortunately, her idea didn't work, because the *Mona Lisa* was painted on wood. Maybe you can write a new solution to the problem: How would the characters steal it?

Trina Schart Hyman

SELECTED TITLES

King Stork
1973

*How Does It Feel
to Be Old?*
1979

*Self-Portrait:
Trina Schart Hyman*
1981

Rapunzel
1982

Little Red Riding Hood
(Caldecott Honor Book)
1983

*Saint George
and the Dragon*
(Caldecott Medal)
1984

*A Child's Christmas
in Wales*
1985

*Hershel and the
Hanukkah Goblins*
(Caldecott Honor Book)
1989

Born:
April 8, 1939, in Philadelphia,
Pennsylvania

Home:
Lyme, New Hampshire

Trina Schart Hyman has always preferred the world of the imagination to the "real world" of shopping malls, newspapers, and television sets.

Growing up in a rural area twenty miles north of Philadelphia, Trina and her younger sister, Karleen, would play games about fairies and imaginary kingdoms. To Trina, "They were more real to us than anything we could really see."

Trina's favorite books were fairy tale, folktale, or mythology collections—anything that could transport her, via her imagination, to a new world. She explains, "It's a chance to take your head and go to another place—another world, another time, another way of feeling."

Perhaps Trina inherited her love of fantasy from her father, a man who loved music, singing, and long walks. "My father told the best stories," Trina wrote in her autobiography, *Self-Portrait: Trina Schart Hyman*. "He sometimes took me for walks at night and told me long magical stories of the origins of the stars. My father's made-up mythology is still much more interesting than the stories the scientists have invented."

A BORN ILLUSTRATOR

Call it an active imagination, a sense of wonder, or simply the ability to dream. Whatever you choose to name it, Trina Schart Hyman was born with a unique talent. She is able to see characters and places in her imagination—and share those visions with others through her art. Illustrating books was the perfect career. Trina confesses, "I don't think I could do anything else. I had to be an artist."

Trina Schart Hyman doesn't believe that a person can decide to become an artist. "Real artists don't say, How do I get to be an artist? That's like saying, Gee, how do I get to have brown eyes. I really think you either are or you aren't." She does, however, offer this advice: "I tell kids to keep on drawing, keep on painting, keep on making pictures. It doesn't matter how you do it; it matters a lot how often you do."

Though Trina has written some books, she mainly works as an illustrator. Once she agrees to illustrate a manuscript—it has to, she says, "ring my chimes"—the work begins. Trina helps the creative process along by taking long walks each morning. She calls it her "thinking time." During these walks, the pictures begin to take shape in her mind. "I don't normally do a lot of sketches because the illustrations and the whole flow of the book are very clear in my head before I start."

But it's never easy to get the pictures out of her mind and onto the paper. Trina admits, "There are some days when I go to sit down at my drawing table and I just want to cry. Sometimes I do cry. But I've learned to keep working—even if I'm messing up and making mistakes."

Trina usually works from ten o'clock in the morning to eight o'clock at night. "If I didn't discipline myself, I just wouldn't work. I'd much rather hang out and fool around. So many people say to me, 'Oh what a fun job, it must be so much fun!' They think I just sort of sit down and goof around.

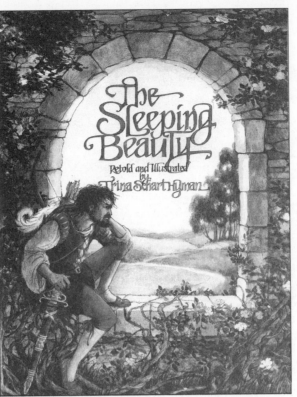

But it's hard work!"

Of her own books, Trina's favorites are *How Does It Feel to Be Old?* and *Little Red Riding Hood. Little Red Riding Hood*, in particular, holds a special place in her heart. The story was a childhood favorite, one her mother used to read aloud to her over and over again.

Trina remembers, "It was so much a part of me that I actually became Little Red Riding Hood. My mother sewed me a red satin cape with a hood that I wore almost every day. My dog, Tippy, was The Wolf."

> "I like kids better than I like grown-ups. They are just a lot easier to talk to and be with. And they are a lot more fun."

SELF-PORTRAIT: *Trina Schart Hyman*

DO IT YOURSELF!

Self-Portrait: Trina Schart Hyman provides readers with interesting information about the artist. Perhaps you'd like to write your own autobiography. Try organizing the information into sections; for example: Home, Family, School, Friends. You decide what to write—it's your life! Just be sure to include illustrations or photographs.

Ezra Jack Keats

SELECTED TITLES

The Snowy Day
(Caldecott Medal)
1962

Whistle for Willie
1964

**John Henry,
an American Legend**
1965

The Little Drummer Boy
1968

Goggles!
(Caldecott Honor Book)
1969

Hi, Cat!
1970

Apt. 3
1971

Over in the Meadow
1971

◆

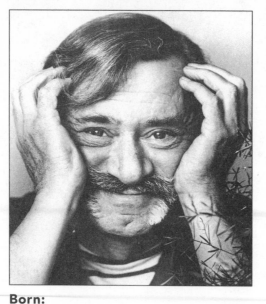

Born:
March 11, 1916, in Brooklyn, New York

Died:
May 6, 1983

When asked where he got his ideas for books, Ezra Jack Keats said with a wink, "Well, as an editor of mine once said, I'm an ex-kid."

In a way, Ezra Jack Keats never did grow up. Even as a man in his sixties, he remembered his childhood as if it were yesterday. He remembered the sights, the sounds, the smells of the city. And his books celebrated the richness, the beauty, and the mystery of a child's life in the city.

Ezra Jack Keats's parents traveled to America from Poland and settled in a poor section of Brooklyn. As a child, he showed an early interest in painting. His mother took great pride in his work. She even let him get away with things that most mothers would not.

"I drew on and colored in everything that came across my path," Ezra Jack Keats said. Once he drew all over his kitchen table. "I filled up the entire table with pictures of little cottages, curly smoke coming out of the chimneys, men's profiles, and kids."

Ezra Jack was happily working away when his mother suddenly entered the room. "I expected her to say, 'What have you been doing?' and 'Get that sponge and wipe it off!' Instead she looked at me and said, 'Did you do that? Isn't it wonderful!' "

His father, however, tried to discourage Ezra Jack from becoming a painter. When Ezra Jack was painting, his father would say, "Get out and play ball and stop making a fool of yourself!" One day he pulled Ezra Jack aside and said, "Never be an artist—you'll have a terrible life."

But Ezra Jack Keats didn't listen. He kept painting away. Slowly, over time, his father realized that Ezra Jack had a special talent. He was so impressed, he took Ezra Jack to The Metropolitan Museum. It would be a day that Ezra Jack would never forget, for it

opened his eyes to the magical possibilities of art. But most important, he learned that his father was proud of his painting.

Keats began his career by illustrating children's books written by other authors. Ezra Jack liked the books he was asked to illustrate. But he was worried. Something, he thought, was missing.

A BLACK HERO

"I never got a story about black people, black children. I decided that if I did a book of my own my hero would be a black child." That book was *The Snowy Day*. It was, according to *Horn Book* magazine, "the very first full-color picture book to feature a small black hero."

It was a simple story, about his own childhood experience. Keats said: "It tells about the excitement I felt as a boy when I woke up to see snow outside the Brooklyn apartment where I grew up."

It really didn't matter whether the star of *The Snowy Day*, Peter, was black or white. The book captured something magical for all children—the wonder and joy of a winter snowfall. Keats remarked, "I had been illustrating books by other people showing the goodness of white children, and in my own book I wanted to show and share the beauty and goodness of the black child."

The Snowy Day won the Caldecott Medal for the best illustrated book of the year. In addition to paint, Keats used scraps of wool, colored paper, scissors and glue to make his beautiful illustrations. This technique is called *collage*.

To make his books, Keats spent days sketching and photographing city streets and children. Then he used these pictures to create his

"The gray background for the pages where Peter goes to sleep (in *The Snowy Day*) was made by splattering India ink with a toothbrush."

illustrations. When he completed the illustrations, he would hang them on his wall. If the characters seemed to be talking to him, he knew the illustrations were right. Ezra Jack Keats believed that good pictures wrote their own stories.

In 1983 Ezra Jack Keats died of a heart attack. But he left his readers with a gift. Books, he told us, should be for all people. He said, "Let us open the book covers to new and wonderful, true and inspiring stories for all children, about all children—the tall and short, fat and thin, dark and light, beautiful and homely. Welcome!"

DO IT YOURSELF!

Study the work of Ezra Jack Keats and then make your own collage using scissors, paper, glue, and paints. Just remember this tip from the artist: "The edges of shapes are varied in several ways. Sharp edges are made by cutting, rough edges by tearing, soft edges by painting over them."

Steven Kellogg

Born:
October 26, 1941, in Norwalk,
Connecticut.

Home:
Sandy Hook, Connecticut

There are few things that
author/illustator Steven
Kellogg enjoys more than
taking his dog, a 180-pound
harlequin Great Dane, on a long
romp through the woods.

Says Kellogg, "The woods are
very relaxing and very peaceful.
Taking walks encourages me to
step inside myself in a calm,
thoughtful way. Just rambling
through the woodland paths,
thinking about stories and
images—it's a good way to make
progress on my work away from
the drawing board."

Surprisingly, Kellogg rarely
takes a sketchbook along with
him. For Steven, it's purely a time
to think, feel, and observe nature.
"I'm always doing visual homework," Kellogg explains. "I know
some artists use models when

they draw, but I don't. But I'm
always storing up images and
expressions in my memory file
that I can flip through and draw
upon when I'm actually working
on a book.

"Part of what artists do is
inspire everyone to be more obser-
vant, to be more aware of the
world around us. Once we take
things for granted, we stop seeing—we stop appreciating the
wonder of the visual world."

When it comes time to work,
Kellogg secludes himself in his
favorite place—a specially
designed studio. "I have a really
terrific room in my house that I
have had for about four years,
though I've dreamed of having it
built for about twenty-five years.
It's at the very top of the house
and it has all sorts of wonderful
roof angles and skylights overlooking the treetops. I love it. It's
like a world of its own."

TELLING STORIES ON PAPER

As a child, Steven loved books
and stories about dinosaurs and
dragons. But he not only enjoyed
reading stories, he also liked making them up. "I had this process,
called telling stories on paper,
where I would make up stories for
my two younger sisters. I scrib-
bled pictures as I talked, sitting
between my sisters with a big
stack of paper on my lap," Kellogg
recalls. Then, laughing, he adds:
"It's essentially what I'm doing
now."

Perhaps because Steven is both
a writer and an illustrator he

believes that words and pictures are equally important. "I think of it as a duet," he says. "Words and pictures are like two voices, singing different melodies. Together, they blend to make it more beautiful, and more meaningful than either voice could be on its own."

But sometimes, Kellogg admits, it can take years to create a book's "beautiful music." That's because Kellogg is a perfectionist. He refuses to let a book go to the publisher before he's completely satisfied. He confesses, "I'm very aware of the fact that once the book is printed, there's no hope for revision. One of my real terrors is to look back at something and think, You should have stuck with that longer; it's not as good as it could have been."

It comes as no surprise, then, to learn that Steven Kellogg revises his work up until the very last moment. No matter how much time he's put into a project he always finds things that can be improved. "I'm constantly rethinking, refining, reworking, rearranging. That's the process by

> "Making a book is like making a friend. You give different sides of yourself to each book, and each book gives different things back to you. Each one is a very special experience."

which the book finds its right momentum from beginning to end."

Young readers often write to Steven Kellogg asking if he likes his job. Steven says, "I relate to

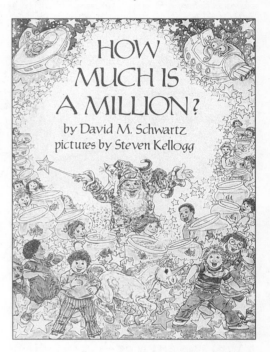

that question very much. As a child I was very aware that many adults hated their jobs. I was determined even then to choose a job that I'd enjoy. When I visit schools, I tell kids that it's important to get to know yourself as well as you can, because then you can choose the job and lifestyle that's right for you."

DO IT YOURSELF!

Steven Kellogg's book *Can I Keep Him?* is about a boy's wish to adopt a pet, any kind of pet: a bear, a lion, even a dinosaur! Try writing a story about what would happen if you were allowed to keep a dinosaur for a pet.

Arnold Lobel

SELECTED TITLES

◆

Born:
May 22, 1933, in Los Angeles, California

Died:
December 4, 1987

The first time Arnold Lobel tried to draw a grasshopper, he failed miserably. He looked at what he drew and thought, *That doesn't look like a grasshopper at all, that looks like a green rabbit!*

But he kept at it, drawing and redrawing his grasshopper. Finally, after much hard work, he succeeded. Today, you can read about Arnold Lobel's grasshopper in the book *Grasshopper on the Road*.

Yes, Arnold Lobel failed at times. But no one worked harder to overcome his failures. His willingness to fail, and then try again, may have been the secret to his success.

Arnold Lobel was born in Los Angeles and grew up in Schenectady, New York. He recalled: "From my house the long walk to the library was downhill all the way. I would return the books I had borrowed and would quickly stock up on five new selections. Five, as I remember, was the most books that one could take out at a time."

He studied fine arts in college and discovered that he had a talent for illustrating books. He also discovered Anita Kempler, a fellow student at Pratt. By graduation they had married, both determined to make it as artists.

Arnold and Anita (who would also earn fame as a children's book illustrator) worked side by side, sharing a drawing table made from an old door.

In 1959, Arnold got his first break. An editor at a publishing house liked a drawing of a cricket that Arnold had made. "Can you draw a salmon?" she asked. Arnold, who had never tried to draw a salmon, said, "Oh yes, I do it all the time!" That day he got a job: illustrating the children's book *Red Tag Comes Home*.

DRAWING UPON HIS LIFE

Lobel believed that a writer or illustrator must draw upon the events in his or her own life. Books, he said, "have to come out of the things that I, as an author, am passionately interested in."

What *did* interest Arnold Lobel? His cat, Orson, for one. Lobel loved his cat. While Arnold worked at his drawing table, Orson would hop right up to rub noses with Arnold. Then Orson would stretch, yawn, and sit down right on top of the illustration Arnold was working on. Maybe that's why cats appear so frequently in his books.

The most famous example of Arnold using his own life as a source for ideas is with the *Frog and Toad* books. While vacationing in Vermont, Lobel's two children returned home with a bucketful of frogs and toads they had caught. Gradually an idea formed for a book about two best friends, a frog and a toad.

Lobel delighted in putting elements of his own life in his books. Read the opening limerick in *A Book of Pigericks* to find out how far he'd go to "put himself" into each story:

> There was an old pig
>   with a pen
> Who wrote stories and verse
>   now and then.
> To enhance these creations,
> He drew illustrations
> With brushes, some paints
>   and his pen.

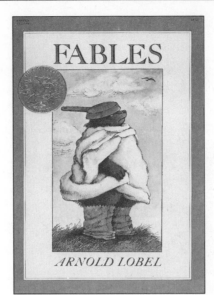

FABLES

ARNOLD LOBEL

"One of the secrets of writing good books for children is that you can't really write books for children; you must write books for yourself and about yourself."

If you look at the illustration on page 8 of that book, you'll see a pig hard at work at a drawing table. Somehow the pig, wearing glasses and a mustache, seems oddly familiar. Now take a look at a picture of Lobel. Notice any similarities? The pig is Arnold Lobel's wacky idea of a self-portrait!

Writing, for Arnold Lobel, was much more difficult than drawing pictures. He said, "Sitting in a chair with an open notebook on my lap, waiting for nothing to happen, is not my idea of fun.

"The creation of most picture books for children is not dramatic," Arnold Lobel said in his acceptance speech for the prestigious Caldecott Medal. "It is a matter of daily, patient, single-minded effort. It is a matter of writing words on a page in a silent room."

Sadly, Arnold Lobel suffered a long illness before he died in December, 1987. Yet he battled his disease each day, creating new books until the very end of his life.

Once, while looking at what he knew would be his last book, *The Turnaround Wind*, Arnold Lobel happily said: "I can't believe I did what I did." Many of his readers have the same reaction: It's hard to believe that one man could be so good.

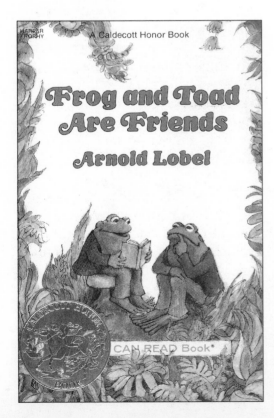

A Caldecott Honor Book

HARPER TROPHY

Frog and Toad Are Friends

Arnold Lobel

CAN READ Book*

DO IT YOURSELF!

In *A Book of Pigericks*, Arnold Lobel took a traditional form of writing (the limerick) and gave it a twist. See if you can write your own pigericks. Or perhaps you'd like to try moosericks or dogericks? Begin by finding out the rules, or proper form, for limericks. If you fail the first time, don't give up. Arnold Lobel never did!

Robert McCloskey

SELECTED TITLES

◆

Born:
September 15, 1914, in Hamilton, Ohio

Home:
Scott Islands, Maine

What's the best way to draw a duck? Well, according to Robert McCloskey, author and illustrator of *Make Way for Ducklings*, "You more or less have to think like a duck!"

And how, you ask, do you think like a duck? Follow some of them around for a few weeks—at least that's what McCloskey did.

When Robert McCloskey was working on the final sketches for *Make Way for Ducklings*, he began to feel dissatisfied with his drawings. He realized, he says, "I really knew very little about them." So early one morning McCloskey visited a poultry dealer in New York. He told the dealer that he would like to buy some mallards. McCloskey remembers, "I was promptly shown a very noisy shipment that had just come in

from the South." That day, Robert McCloskey returned home to his apartment toting four live ducks.

The tiny apartment was pure chaos, filled with waddling, quacking ducks. "I spent the next weeks on my hands and knees, armed with a box of Kleenex and a sketchbook, following ducks around the studio and observing them in the bathtub."

As the weeks passed, McCloskey was even able to think like a duck. He says, "No effort is too great to find out as much as possible about the things you are drawing. It's a good feeling to be able to put down a line and know that it is right."

As this story illustrates, McCloskey is something of a perfectionist. If a drawing isn't exactly right, he'll rip it up and start all over. He says, "There are sometimes as many as twenty or thirty drawings before I turn out the one you see in the book—not completed drawings, of course, but ones finding out and exploring the best possible way of presenting a particular picture."

A "SERIOUS" ARTIST

Robert McCloskey grew up in the small town of Hamilton, Ohio. As a child he took piano lessons and learned to play the harmonica, the drums, and the oboe. He had thought that he would become a musician until he discovered electronics. He loved to tinker with old electric motors and clocks, pulling them apart and trying to put them together again. He even invented a revolving Christmas tree.

Eventually, McCloskey decided to become a "serious" artist. "My mind in those days," McCloskey recalled, "was filled with odd bits of Greek mythology—Spanish galleons, Oriental dragons, and all the stuff that really and truly great art is made of."

For two entire summers, he lived on Cape Cod and made paintings. But no one bought them. McCloskey confesses, "My career was a bust."

Thanks to a conversation with an editor, McCloskey decided to rethink his career. The editor looked at McCloskey's paintings of mythological figures, dragons, and winged horses and gently suggested that he try creating more realistic images. Her comments

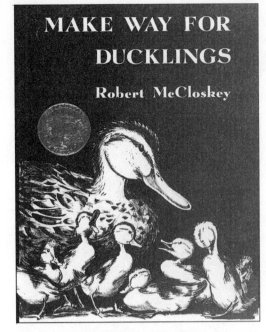

made him think about growing up in Ohio and the ordinary events of his childhood. Instead of painting fantasies, McCloskey decided to focus on everyday life.

McCloskey's first book, *Lentil*, sprang from his own childhood experiences. His next book was *Make Way for Ducklings*, which is one of the most famous, best-loved books in the history of children's literature. McCloskey first noticed ducklings years earlier when he used to walk through the Boston Public Garden on his way

to art school. But at the time, he says, "It never occurred to me to *draw* those things."

By focusing on ordinary life, Robert McCloskey created many successful books. *Blueberries for Sal*, *One Morning in Maine*, *A Time of Wonder*, and *Burt Dow, Deep-Water Man* were all inspired by the experience of living part of each year on an island off the coast of Maine. "Living on an island is lots of fun and lots of work," he says. "In the spring when we first arrive, there are boats to paint, a garden to plant, the float and dock to repair, dead trees to cut down, and a thousand other things to do. But when it's a nice day, we stop our work to go fishing or sailing or picnicking."

> **"Like a musician who likes to have his music listened to, I like to have my pictures looked at and enjoyed."**

DO IT YOURSELF!

Robert McCloskey believes that you have to know something very well in order to draw it well. Do you think that's true? Try this experiment. Draw a picture of a cat using your imagination. Then study a live cat for a few days and draw it again. Which picture is better: the first drawing or the second?

James Marshall

SELECTED TITLES

George and Martha
1972

The Stupids Step Out
1974

Mary Alice, Operator Number 9
1975

Miss Nelson Is Missing!
1977

Portly McSwine
1979

Red Riding Hood
1987

Goldilocks and the Three Bears
(Caldecott Honor Book)
1988

Born:
October 10, 1942, in San Antonio, Texas

Home:
Mansfield Hollow, Connecticut, and New York, New York

Ideas for James Marshall's books usually begin with daydreams and doodles. While sketching, Marshall has been known to discover some very interesting characters. He explains, "The story develops out of the character's personality. For me, as an illustrator, it often comes from what will look funny. The idea of a character pouring soup into his loafers is a funny kind of thing. It's visually funny. The words come to me later."

Still, James Marshall is reluctant to claim that he completely understands the creative process. "An author or illustrator can point out the mysteries, or the magic, or even the silliness of the world. But to me, it doesn't come out of the author; the author explores something that already exists. I didn't make up the things that are funny in my books. I just see them, recognize them, and pass them along. It doesn't really matter where the ideas come from."

Like the work of all great illustrators, there is no mistaking Marshall's work for anyone else's. You look at a plump hippopotamus lazily lounging in a tub and you know it can only be the work of Marshall.

Part of the reason James Marshall has a unique style is because he is a self-taught artist. "I'm glad that I never went to art school," he says, "because had I gone I probably would have ended up copying the style of other illustrators. People love a Maurice Sendak or an Arnold Lobel book because of the special, very individual vision they bring to their work. This is why the artists I love are not the cool technicians but those who have a vision to share with others."

ALMOST NORMAL

James Marshall was born and raised in Texas. He lived on a sprawling, eighty-five-acre farm outside of San Antonio. He was an only child until he was twelve years old. As a result, Marshall reflects, "like many children who are alone a great deal, I had to fall back on my own resources. I lived in my imagination."

Marshall's childhood was almost normal. He did, however, have one peculiar habit: "My sister recently reminded me that as a kid I used to hide toast. I hated toast. So instead of eating it, I would hide it. The closet in my bedroom was stacked with toast!"

Today, Marshall divides his time between two homes—one in Mansfield Hollow, Connecticut, and one in Manhattan. He does most of his work in his Connecticut studio. But there's always a sketchbook nearby in case he gets in a creative mood.

"The real trick,"Marshall confides, "is to find your own personal working rhythms—your own way of working."

While many illustrators keep conventional hours, working from nine to five, Marshall prefers to work at night—sometimes in the wee, small hours. "The later, the better," he claims. "My ideas are usually fresher and funnier at night."

What does James Marshall con-

sider the hardest part of creating a picture book? "It's always the ending that gives me the most trouble," Marshall admits. "The ending," he says, "is what people remember. If the book fizzles at the end, they remember the whole thing as a fizzled book. It's important to have a very satisfying ending for the reader. They've entered a world and now they are leaving it. So it's a puzzle that has to be solved. I remember with one of the *Miss Nelson* books it took us (the author Harry Allar and I) two years to come up with an ending we liked!"

> ## "If I don't have a good character, then I don't have a book."

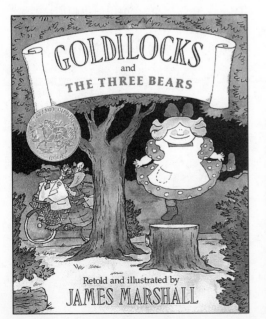

DO IT YOURSELF!

James Marshall believes that reading enriches the imagination. Asked to suggest an activity that will help kids enjoy his books, Marshall said, "I'd like to see kids read my books, then sit back and just daydream. After all, daydreaming is important — I've practically made a career out of it." Sounds like good advice indeed. Ready, set, daydream!

Robert Munsch

SELECTED TITLES

Mud Puddle
1979

The Paper Bag Princess
1980

Murmel, Murmel, Murmel
1982

Thomas' Snowsuit
1985

Love You Forever
1986

A Promise Is a Promise
1988

Angela's Airplane
1988

Giant
1989

◆

Born:
June 11, 1945, in Pittsburgh, Pennsylvania

Home:
Guelph, Ontario, Canada

Although he is the author of more than twenty books, Robert Munsch doesn't know a lot about the writing process. That's because he tells his stories out loud. It isn't until after he's told his stories—in some cases, as many as one hundred times—that Robert finally gets around to writing them down. Munsch concedes, "I got into it backwards."

FIVE HUNDRED AND NINETEEN STORIES

While working in a day-care center for young children, Robert Munsch began telling stories for very practical reasons. He recalls, "I found that I could get kids to shut up at nap time by telling them stories. I worked out this deal where the kids could ask me for one story that I'd already told and I would also make up a new one. At that time, I wasn't thinking of being a writer. But the trick was, by letting them ask for only one old story, they only asked for the good ones. The first day-care center where I did that, I made up 519 stories over two years."

Out of those 519 stories, Munsch found that the children requested only about ten of them over and over again. He says, "After two years, I left there with ten good stories."

The revision process for Munsch, unlike most writers who sit alone in a room reworking their stories, comes through repeated tellings. "When I first start telling them," Munsch confides, "they change wildly—whole plots, characters, everything is up for grabs. Once the stories get steady, then it's just little dinky things that change."

But Munsch doesn't think too much about revision and editing. When he's telling his stories, the changes come about naturally.

Robert explains, "When I'm performing in front of forty kids, I'm not thinking like a writer. I'm thinking like a performer. I just want to keep them happy."

You could say that Robert Munsch is a walking, talking, story machine. But where in the world does he get all those ideas? That's a question that Munsch doesn't particularly like. "People are always asking, 'Where do you get your ideas?' as if somehow that were the essence. It's not. It's part of the essence. Lots of people have good ideas for books. I have lots of good ideas for books. So what?

"Ideas are cheap; books are expensive. I have no trouble getting ideas. It's books I have trouble getting. There are lots of times when I know I have a good story idea, but it takes me years to actually get a good story. A recent book of mine, *Something Good*, is about going shopping. I've been trying to do a good shopping story for ten years. I knew the idea was good, but that doesn't necessarily mean a book will happen."

Robert Munsch confesses that it took him a while to learn how to make the transition from *teller* to *writer*. At first, he says, "I made the mistake of attempting to change my stories into what I considered to be good writing. They were terrible." Eventually, Munsch figured out that the closer he came to reproducing the spoken version, the better the story would be.

For a story to be worthy of becoming a book, it must pass a series of tests. Munsch explains, "When I get a story that's good, I try to drag it through all kinds of situations. My rule's Urban/Rural: tell it in the city, tell it in the

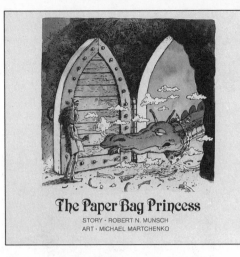

The Paper Bag Princess
STORY · ROBERT N. MUNSCH
ART · MICHAEL MARTCHENKO

country. And in Canada, North/South—tell it in southern Canada and then take it way up into the Arctic. If I can get a story that floats in all those places, it's got to be a pretty good story."

Robert Munsch also finds that some of his stories succeed in some places and fail in others. "Sometimes a story isn't publishable simply because it's too tightly woven into one particular community," he says. "I have lots of stories that I've told for Inuit communities up North that work really well in a community where people hunt for a living and eat raw caribou. But they don't work in Toronto because nobody there hunts for a living, and they *certainly* don't eat raw caribou!"

"Kids either keep laughing, or, if they don't like the story, they get up and leave. That's the honest feedback I depend on."

DO IT YOURSELF!

Robert Munsch says that he makes up most of his stories on the spot. He calls it thinking on his feet. Why not give it a try. Pick a friend and say, "I'm going to make up a story about you." And then give it a try.

Jerry Pinkney

Born:
December 22, 1939, in Philadelphia, Pennsylvania

Home:
Croton-on-Hudson, New York

"**A** successful illustration," states artist Jerry Pinkney, "starts with a good manuscript."

Judging from the success of Jerry's illustrations, he's worked on some very fine manuscripts indeed. "I've been very fortunate," Jerry says. "Actually, it's amazing! Because with my success, I'm now getting even *better* manuscripts to work from."

Almost every day, Jerry receives a new manuscript in the mail. It's difficult to decide which ones to illustrate. For Jerry—first and foremost—the manuscript must reach him on an emotional level. Jerry explains, "I'm looking, first of all, for an exciting story to work on. At that point, it really has nothing to do with whether it's a good story, in terms of how

well it's written. I'm only responding to it in terms of illustrations. Only after the second or third go-round do I begin to think, Hey, this story is really well written!"

The manuscript must pass other tests. Jerry says, "I ask myself, Is there really a good, strong reason to do the book? Is there really a chance to do something that's important to me? Certainly in the case of African-American stories, I'm drawn to them because there's such a need for those books. But that's also true of a story that might be about a Spanish kid, or a story about Native Americans. Then there's always one last thing to consider," Jerry says with a laugh. "Whether the project can fit into my crazy schedule."

A UNIQUE APPROACH

Jerry Pinkney uses drawing as a way to *see* his ideas. It's as if he doesn't know exactly what he thinks until the pencil hits the paper. Jerry tries to explain, "I don't see things until I draw them. When I put a line down, the only thing I know is how it should feel, and I know when it doesn't feel right.

"I'm not one who sits right down and does a lot of sketching at first. I work best by thinking about an assignment for awhile, jotting down notes as ideas come to me. Then I do a few rough thumbnail sketches. These sketches help me figure out correct composition and how to set up situations."

During the early stages of Jerry's creative process, he "wallows in reference material." That's because Jerry likes to makes his drawings as true-to-life as possible. Jerry points out, "If you look at the books, the clothing and setting are very researched. I try to set my stories in a specific time and place. In a way, it's like theater. I'm trying to build a set for these characters."

If Jerry Pinkney's characters look lifelike to you, they should. Jerry often asks live models to act out the story while he takes photographs. Then he uses the photographs when he draws the final illustrations.

"The models I choose help bring out my characters' inner life. When I find a model that has the physical attributes I want in a character, I pose and direct him or her in ways that pull out the character I'm looking for. When I work with models that happen to be children, I have them read the manuscript. Then we act the story out together."

Jerry Pinkney feels that models are essential to his particular style

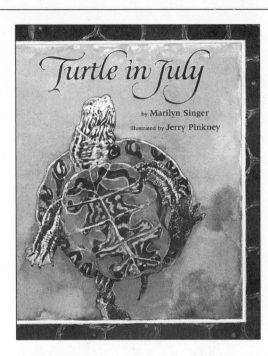

Turtle in July
by Marilyn Singer
illustrated by Jerry Pinkney

"My work has allowed me to dream."

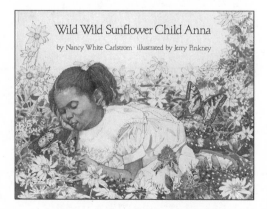

Wild Wild Sunflower Child Anna
by Nancy White Carlstrom   illustrated by Jerry Pinkney

of working. "My work is fairly realistic," he says. "Gestures of the hands, for example, cannot just come out of my head. I really need that figure responding in front of me."

After a drawing has been approved by an art director, Jerry is ready, like a sprinter, to "go to the finish." Jerry says that this is the most difficult part of the process, because now all decisions are final. The setting, the clothes, the gestures, the colors, the style—every detail must be exactly right. It's hard, hard work. But there are magical times when everything goes perfectly. "If that particular painting gives back what you have in your head, then it's magical," Jerry Pinkney says. "There are times when pictures sort of take off on their own. Illustrating books can be a wonderful experience!"

DO IT YOURSELF!

The Canadian goose is Jerry Pinkney's favorite illustration from *Turtle in July*. For Jerry, the struggle was to make the goose seem alive. He solved the problem by drawing the goose with its leg lifted up and its neck twisted around. Make your own animal drawing. But, like Jerry Pinkney, be sure to give it some gesture or movement that makes it come alive!

Barbara Reid

SELECTED TITLES

The New Baby Calf
1984

Have You Seen Birds?
1987

Sing a Song of Mother Goose
1989

Effie
1990

◆

Born:
November 16, 1957, in Toronto, Ontario, Canada

Home:
Toronto, Ontario, Canada

According to Barbara Reid, coming up with the idea for an illustration can take anywhere from five minutes to five weeks. She explains, "With some pages I know from the beginning exactly what I want to do. With other pages I can walk around for days accomplishing nothing. It's really frustrating. I clean the house, I shop, I reorganize cupboards. I do all kinds of stuff just to avoid dealing with it. Then an idea comes somehow."

"When I visit kids," Barbara says, "I try to give them an idea of what it's like to be an illustrator. It seems easy if you look at someone's finished illustrations. But if you read the manuscript on a bare, typewritten page, then you realize what an illustrator has to do to help bring a story to life."

When Barbara is searching for the right way to illustrate a manuscript, she'll often surround herself with pictures, clippings, and reference books. It's as if she's preparing the house for an invited guest—in this case, an idea—to come visit. Barbara explains, "I just lay out all the possibilities for an idea to come in, and then I wait."

PLAYING WITH PLASTICINE

Readers first began to appreciate Barbara's talent with the publication of *The New Baby Calf*. In it, Barbara selected an unusual technique to create the pictures—she used Plasticine, the same stuff that many kids play with in preschool.

Barbara thinks that with a little effort, just about anybody can create a good picture using Plasticine. "Plasticine is friendly," she says with a laugh. "You can watch the most serious people in the world sit down at a table and slowly they'll start twiddling with it. Suddenly they are having a great time, very involved in making a dinosaur. It's like ice cream: everybody likes it."

Barbara also enjoys working with Plasticine because it never completely hardens. This allows her to keep adding bits and pieces to her pictures. She describes the process: "I'll look at an illustration and at the last minute I'll stick on a bug or something because the picture seems to need it. That's the really fun part. Sometimes it ends up being one of

Noah's Ark right now. I like doing traditional things. It's a fun challenge, taking something that is well known and interpreting it. As a basis for the text, I'm using an old folk song that everyone knows. Even though the story is from the Bible, I'm focusing on the humor of it—the ark filling up, the incredible mess, and all those animals to count."

Barbara has a deep respect for the words in a story. She says, "You see some books that have been around for a million years with crummy illustrations. But it's the story that people keep coming back to." She adds, firmly, "The story is the most important part."

Since Barbara Reid doesn't usually write her own books, she must choose her stories from among the manuscripts that are sent to her by editors. Barbara confesses, "It's a big responsibility. I don't want to do any old book. I want to do something really good, and I don't always know how to find it. That's my dream, to find that wonderful story."

the most important parts of the picture, because it gives the illustration that little kick."

When choosing a project, Barbara is attracted to new challenges, new ways to grow as an artist. She says, "I guess I get interested if it's something I haven't done before. I don't like to be repetitive."

After *Have You Seen Birds?*, Barbara tried her hand at nursery rhymes with *Sing a Song of Mother Goose*. Barbara enjoyed the change. "I'd never had a chance to illustrate costumes before," she says. "Birds and calves are dressed as they're dressed and you can't play around with it. With *Mother Goose*, I worked in all kinds of colors. It's so much more exciting to do faces than beaks."

Barbara's newest challenge will be to write her first picture book. "I'm working on a story about

> **"I'm doing the same thing now that I've done since I was four. I read a story and then make a picture of it. I've been lucky."**

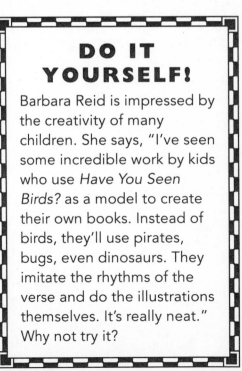

DO IT YOURSELF!

Barbara Reid is impressed by the creativity of many children. She says, "I've seen some incredible work by kids who use *Have You Seen Birds?* as a model to create their own books. Instead of birds, they'll use pirates, bugs, even dinosaurs. They imitate the rhythms of the verse and do the illustrations themselves. It's really neat." Why not try it?

Maurice Sendak

SELECTED TITLES

◆

Born:
June 10, 1928, in Brooklyn, New York

Home:
Ridgefield, Connecticut

Maurice Sendak believes that children live in two worlds—fantasy and reality. *Where the Wild Things Are*, his acclaimed masterpiece, reflects that belief. Max, the hero of the book, moves from reality to fantasy and back to reality again. Sendak comments, "Through fantasy, Max discharges his anger against his mother and returns to the real world sleepy, hungry, and at peace with himself."

Sendak believes that it's important for children to have a lively imagination. And for an artist it is essential. "Fantasy is the core of all writing for children, as I think it is for the writing of any book, for any creative act, perhaps for the act of living," he says. "But these fantasies have to be given physical form so you build a house around them. And the

house is what you call a story. And the painting of the house is the bookmaking. But essentially it's a dream or a fantasy."

Make no mistake: Sendak's fantasy stories are about real life. His books often deal with everyday feelings such as anger and fear. Some critics believe the books are too frightening for young children. Sendak disagrees: "Children know a lot more than people give them credit for. Children are willing to deal with many dubious subjects that grown-ups think they shouldn't know about. But children are small, courageous people who have to deal every day with a multitude of problems, just as we adults do."

THE INFLUENCE OF EARLY DAYS

Perhaps more than any artist, Maurice Sendak draws his inspiration from memories of his early childhood. For example, *In the Night Kitchen* was inspired by an advertisement Sendak remembered from childhood. He recalls, "The advertisement was for the Sunshine Bakers. And the advertisement read, 'We Bake While You Sleep!'"

The advertisement angered young Maurice a great deal. He wanted to stay up all night to see what the grown-ups did! "I remember I used to save the coupons showing the three fat little Sunshine bakers going off to this yummy place, wherever it was, to have their fun, while I had to go to bed. The book was a way

WHERE THE WILD THINGS ARE

STORY AND PICTURES BY MAURICE SENDAK

to get back at them and say that now I'm old enough to stay up late and see what's going on in the night kitchen."

Sendak drew upon a childhood fear for his favorite book, *Outside Over There*. "Much of it is based

OUTSIDE OVER THERE
MAURICE SENDAK

"Writing is very difficult and gives me a great deal of pleasure, partly because it is so difficult."

on what scared me when I was little. I remember as a very small child seeing a book about a little girl who is caught in a rainstorm. She's wearing a huge yellow slicker and boots. The rain comes down harder and harder and begins to rise and spill into her boots, and that's when I would

always stop looking at the book. It scared me too much. I never found out what happened to the little girl."

A sickly boy, Maurice did not have a happy childhood. He remembers, "I was miserable as a kid, I couldn't make friends. I couldn't play stoopball, I couldn't skate. I stayed home and drew pictures. When I wanted to go out and do something, my father would say, 'You'll catch a cold.' And I did. I did whatever he told me."

When he was a child, Maurice withdrew into a life of fantasy. And he fed his fantasy life with books. "As a child," he says, "I felt that books were holy objects, to be caressed, rapturously sniffed, and devotedly provided for. I gave my life to them. I still do. I continue to do what I did as a child—dream of books, make books, and collect books."

Today, Maurice Sendak values the fact that his readers are children. What he likes most about children is their honesty. "I long ago discovered that they make the best audience. They certainly make the best critics," Sendak said. "When children love your book, it's 'I love your book, thank you, I want to marry you when I grow up.' Or it's 'Dear Mr. Sendak: I hate your book. Hope you die soon. Cordially.' "

DO IT YOURSELF!

Your dreams are like messages from the imagination. Leave paper and a pen beside your bed. When you wake in the morning, try to remember your dreams. Before getting up, spend a few minutes writing them down. Who knows? These dreams might inspire a fantastic story some day.

Dr. Seuss (Theodor Seuss Geisel)

SELECTED TITLES

And To Think I Saw It on Mulberry Street
1937

Horton Hatches the Egg
1940

Bartholomew and the Oobleck
(Caldecott Honor Book)
1949

If I Ran the Zoo
(Caldecott Honor Book)
1950

The Cat in the Hat
1957

How the Grinch Stole Christmas
1957

Yertle the Turtle and Other Stories
1958

Green Eggs and Ham
1960

The Lorax
1971

The Butter Battle Book
1984

◆

Born:
March 2, 1904, in Springfield, Massachusetts

Home:
La Jolla, California

Where does Dr. Seuss get all of his wonderfully wacky ideas? "I get all my ideas in Switzerland near the Forka Pass," Dr. Seuss once explained. "There is a little town called Gletch, and two thousand feet up above Gletch there is a smaller hamlet called Über Gletch. I go there on the fourth of August every summer to get my cuckoo clock repaired. While the cuckoo is in the hospital, I wander around and talk to the people in the streets. They are very strange people, and I get my ideas from them."

Of course, Seuss isn't serious. But he is seriously poking fun at the notion that authors can ever really know where their ideas come from. That's the way the mind of Dr. Seuss works: He often uses nonsense to make an important point.

"Anything can spark an idea," Seuss claims. And believe it or not, once an idea blew in through an open window. Seuss was at his drawing table, aimlessly doodling. Suddenly, a gentle breeze blew a drawing he had made of an elephant on top of another drawing he had made of a tree. Seuss remembers, "I said to myself, an elephant in a tree! What's he doing there? Finally I said to myself, Of course! He's hatching an egg!" Seuss had discovered the idea for his next book, *Horton Hatches an Egg*.

Doodling is a favorite technique Seuss uses to conjure up ideas. For example, he once drew a picture of a turtle sitting on top of another turtle. Seuss kept drawing until there was a huge pile of turtles stacked one on top of the other. He looked at the preposterous pile of turtles and asked himself, Why? What does this mean? (To discover how Seuss answered the question, you'll have to read the book he wrote in 1958 entitled *Yertle the Turtle and Other Stories*!)

PURE NONSENSE. . .OR IS IT?

You should know that Dr. Seuss isn't the author's real name; it's a pseudonym invented by the writer. His real name is Theodor Seuss Geisel (pronounced "GUY-zel"). There isn't a more famous children's author in the entire world. His books are witty, weird, wacky, wild, and wonderful. But most of all, they are read and read and read again. Today there are more than 200 million copies of Dr. Seuss's books in print. And those books are translated into seventeen languages.

Seuss has invented some of the strangest, most memorable characters in all literature. There's Horton, Bartholomew Cubbins, The Zooks and the Sneetches, the Grinch and the Cat in the Hat, the Tufted Gustard, and the lovable Lorax!

How does he come up with all those weird names? "That's the easy part," Seuss says. "I can look at an animal and know what it is."

Dr. Seuss often uses silly characters and strange lands as a way of talking about real-life, serious issues. His books have addressed

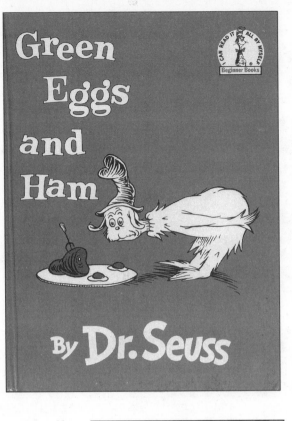

"Nonsense wakes up the brain cells."

important topics such as nuclear weapons (*The Butter Battle Book*), protecting the environment (*The Lorax*), and prejudice (*The Sneetches and Other Stories*).

Seuss's interest in animals blossomed when he was just a little boy and his father ran a zoo in Massachusetts. Seuss would visit with a sketchpad, stand outside the cages, and draw all the animals. Of course, he drew them his own way! Seuss admits, "I can't draw real animals. I'm a cartoonist, not an artist."

For Seuss, there's little difference between kids and adults. He said, "I feel the same about kids as I do about adults—some are delightful, some are dreadful. Most writers of kids' books will tell you all children are wonderful, but they're not."

Though his wife, Audrey, has two children from a previous marriage, Dr. Seuss never had any children of his own. Why no kids for the famous children's book author? Seuss says, thinking of his many readers, "I have 200 million kids. That's enough."

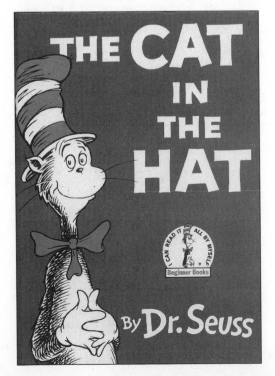

DO IT YOURSELF!

Dr. Seuss often gets ideas by doodling. He'll draw a picture and then ask himself, Why? How did this happen? Then he invents a story to explain it. You can try that too. If you don't like to draw, you can always look at pictures in magazines. Find an interesting picture that strikes your fancy. Then make up a story.

William Steig

SELECTED TITLES

CDB!
1968

Sylvester and the Magic Pebble
(Caldecott Medal)
1969

Dominic
1972

The Amazing Bone
(Caldecott Medal)
1976

Abel's Island
(Newbery Award)
1976

Caleb and Kate
1977

Tiffky Doofky
1978

Doctor De Soto
(Newbery Honor Book)
1982

Spinky Sulks
1988

◆

Born:
November 14, 1907, in New York, New York

Home:
Kent, Connecticut

Writing and illustrating books isn't a very complicated process for William Steig. Steig explains, "I begin by deciding it's time to write a book. And then I think about what animal I will use. It takes a while before things start happening. I can't truly say that I am ever inspired to write a book. It's the last thing in the world I think of until I have to do it. And then I count on my imagination to make things happen."

William Steig's imagination seems to be in good shape, because things certainly do happen in his books. In fact, pretty much *anything* can happen: a man is turned into a dog (*Caleb and Kate*); a donkey finds a magic pebble (*Sylvester and the Magic Pebble*); a bone talks and casts magic spells (*The Amazing Bone*); and a boa constrictor named Dolores falls in love with a garbage collector (*Tiffky Doofky*). Steig says, "I just ramble around and discover for myself what will happen next."

William Steig believes in working quickly. "I want to get it out of the way," he says. For him, too much thinking only gets in the way of his imagination. He once said, "It's only when you're consciously aware of what you're doing in a book that you're in trouble." The book *Caleb and Kate* is typical of the way he works. Steig recalls, "The only thing I set out with was the idea of a man being transformed into a dog, which I thought would be fun to work with."

A LATE BLOOMER

William Steig grew up in a creative household, where artistic and musical pursuits were encouraged. As a child, he loved to read books; *Robinson Crusoe*, *Robin Hood*, and *Pinocchio* were his favorites. *Robinson Crusoe*, in particular, seems to have had a lasting effect. In a way, *Abel's Island* is Steig's own version of Robinson Crusoe's adventures; except in this case, the stranded castaway is a mouse named Adelard Hassam di Chirico Flint.

Steig began his career as a cartoonist. The year was 1930, and the country was in the throes of the Great Depression. To help support his family, Steig sold his first cartoon to *The New Yorker* magazine. It was the beginning of a long relationship; you can still find cartoons by William Steig in current issues of *The New Yorker*.

As the years passed, Steig found a job in advertising. But, he says, he "detested" it. Fortunately, in 1967, children's author Robert Kraus suggested that Steig try his hand at writing children's books. Steig jumped at the opportunity because he saw it as a way to leave advertising. His first book for children, *CDB!*, was soon published. And a new career had begun.

Although William Steig's illustrations have been widely praised, it is his way with words that readers seem to enjoy most. He uses all sorts of long, outrageous words, like *cantankerous* and *recumbent*. He also uses made-up words, such as *dramberaber-oomed* and *jibrakken sibibble digray*.

William Steig respects the intelligence of kids—that's why he doesn't hesitate to use long words in his stories. He also believes that adults have a lot to learn from children. But he's not sentimental and gushy about kids. He once

> "Writing is fun. I really enjoy that. I think writing's a good career. If you write, you discover things about yourself in the process."

said, "Every kid is a potential genius, but also a potential yucka-puck." (And although no one besides William Steig is quite sure what *yuckapuck* means, it probably isn't very nice.)

Of course, William Steig's career in children's books almost didn't happen. He never intended to become an author and illustrator. He once said, "If I'd had it my way, I'd have been a professional athlete, a sailor, a beachcomber or some other form of hobo, a painter, a gardener, a novelist, a banjo player, a traveler."

But for William Steig, life—like books—can't be planned in advance. Perhaps that's what he had in mind when he wrote *Dominic*. In the book, a dog sets out to see more of the world. Soon, Dominic must choose between two paths: a road with "no surprise, nothing to discover or wonder at" or another road, which promises to lead him to "where things will happen that you never could have guessed at— marvelous, unbelievable things."

Like his creator, Dominic chose the second path: the one of surprise and adventure, the one where anything can happen. Even writing your first children's book at the age of sixty!

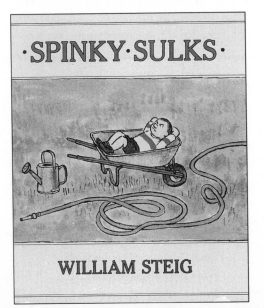

DO IT YOURSELF!

When William Steig can't find the perfect word to describe a smell, sound, sight, or feeling, he makes one up. You won't find *dramberamberoomed* in any dictionary, but that doesn't mean there's a better way to describe a loud crash of thunder. Follow William Steig's example by making up words of your own. Be sure to write out clear definitions for them. Use each of the new words in a sentence. Read the sentences to a friend. You'll have a fantaburiffic time!

John Steptoe

SELECTED TITLES

Stevie
1969

Uptown
1970

Train Ride
1971

Daddy Is a Monster...Sometimes
1980

All the Colors of the Race: Poems
1982

The Story of Jumping Mouse: A Native American Legend
(Caldecott Honor Book)
1984

Mufaro's Beautiful Daughters: An African Tale
(Caldecott Honor Book)
1987

Born:
September 14, 1950, in Brooklyn, New York

Died:
August 28, 1989

At age nineteen, John Lewis Steptoe came to national attention when his first book, *Stevie*, was hailed by *Life* magazine as "a new kind of book for black children."

Stevie was one of the first children's books to focus on black life in the ghetto. The colors of its illustrations were vibrant and alive; the words crackled with life and energy.

In the book, Robert, an only child, must suddenly share his home with a smaller boy, Stevie. Listen to the words Steptoe used to describe Robert's first reaction to Stevie: "And so Stevie moved in with his old cry-baby self. He always had to have his way. And he was greedy too. Everything he sees he wants. 'Could I have somma that? Gimme this.' Man!"

In an interview with *The New York Times Book Review*, Steptoe commented, "I wrote the book for black children, therefore the language reflects it. I think black children need this. I wrote it this way because they are never spoken to. They always read about themselves as 'the Negro'—someone outside, not included."

John Steptoe did not have to look far for story ideas. Almost all of his sixteen books explore family and city life. And why not—John grew up in an apartment building in the Bedford-Stuyvesant section of Brooklyn, with parents, two brothers, and a sister.

GROWTH AND CHANGE

"I love to change and grow," Steptoe said. And that is exactly what he did throughout his career. Although he illustrated his early books with lively, vibrant colors, Steptoe shifted to using only black ink, pencil, or charcoal. It was his way of challenging himself as an illustrator. The restricted use of color forced him to become a better draftsperson. The culmination of this period came with his book *The Story of Jumping Mouse*.

The Story of Jumping Mouse was a Native American legend about a mouse who dreams of reaching a better, more beautiful world in "a far-off land." When John Steptoe first discovered the legend, he saw in the mouse character his own hopes and dreams for a better world. He said, "I heard this story several years ago, and it has always haunted me. It spoke to me about things that I would like to say to children."

John Steptoe's greatest success came in 1987; after two-and-a-half years of work and research, he published *Mufaro's Beautiful Daughters*. It, too, was named a Caldecott Honor Book. And in *Mufaro's Beautiful Daughters*, all of John Steptoe's talents came together. Once again, he returned to the bright colors of his youth. But his illustrations were better somehow—richer, warmer, and more interesting. All of his years refining his craft had paid off.

Mufaro's Beautiful Daughters, dedicated to the children of South Africa, is based on an African folktale. In this fable, John found a

STEVIE

JOHN STEPTOE

new way to express his pride in his African heritage.

In his acceptance speech for the Caldecott award he had won, Steptoe told the audience, "The award gives me hope that children who are still caught in the frustration of being black and poor in America will be encouraged to love themselves enough to accomplish the dreams I know are in

their hearts."

On August 28, 1989, John Steptoe died of AIDS. He was 38 years old. No one can know whether John Steptoe, like Jumping Mouse, ever reached a more beautiful world in a "far-off land." But through his books, many readers continue to be inspired by his hopes and dreams for a better world.

"The more I read, the more reasons I found to be proud of my African ancestors."

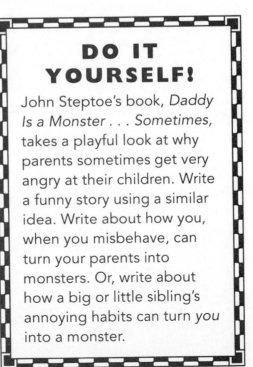

DO IT YOURSELF!

John Steptoe's book, *Daddy Is a Monster . . . Sometimes,* takes a playful look at why parents sometimes get very angry at their children. Write a funny story using a similar idea. Write about how you, when you misbehave, can turn your parents into monsters. Or, write about how a big or little sibling's annoying habits can turn *you* into a monster.

Chris Van Allsburg

SELECTED TITLES

The Garden of Abdul Gasazi
(Caldecott Honor Book)
1979

Jumanji
(Caldecott Medal)
1981

Ben's Dream
1982

The Wreck of the Zephyr
1983

The Mysteries of Harris Burdick
1984

The Polar Express
(Caldecott Medal)
1985

The Stranger
1986

The Z Was Zapped: A Play in Twenty-Six Acts
1987

Just a Dream
1990

◆

Born:
June 18, 1949, in Grand Rapids, Michigan

Home:
Providence, Rhode Island

A boy, in bed, floats high above the treetops. A sailboat lifts off the water and flies among the clouds. And on a snowy winter's night, a train mysteriously pauses on a quiet street.

Welcome to the world of Chris Van Allsburg—a world of mystery, magic, and strange beauty. It is a world where, in Chris's words, "strange things may happen."

Though Chris doesn't know where his ideas come from, he does admit that his stories usually evolve from a single illustration. He says, "I start with an image, and I know there must be a story that makes sense of it."

Try to imagine Chris Van Allsburg working in his large studio in Providence, Rhode Island. There he is: drawing aimlessly, just creating images on paper. Puzzled, he stops to look at the picture in front of him. It may be a haunting illustration of a train in front of a house. Somehow, the picture creates questions in Chris's mind. How did the train get there? Where is it going? Why?

At that exact moment—when Chris begins to ask questions—the process of creating the story begins. He becomes a detective, searching for clues. Only a story can solve the mystery of a picture.

Van Allsburg remarks, "It almost seems like a discovery, as if the story was always there. The few elements I start out with are actually clues. If I figure out what they mean, I can discover the story that's waiting."

That process is exactly how Chris "discovered" *The Polar Express*. He thought about the boy and the train. In his imagination, he got on the train to see where it would lead him. He recalls, "The train kept rolling all the way to the North Pole."

LIKE MAKING MOVIES

Chris Van Allsburg was already a successful sculptor when he began writing and illustrating books for children. Oddly enough, it all happened because he didn't want to watch TV. Chris remembers, "I began drawing little pictures—it was either that or watch TV. My wife thought they'd appeal to kids. I wrote a little story, and that became my first book."

Sound easy? It isn't. It takes a lot of hard work. Chris says, "A book is a four-and-a-half-month commitment, and the challenge is to actually finish it." One of Chris's problems is that he gets too many ideas. He confesses, "I've got a sketchbook in my head with thousands of pieces of sculpture and enough descriptions for ten books. I would like to be six people at once, so that I could get more of them out of the way."

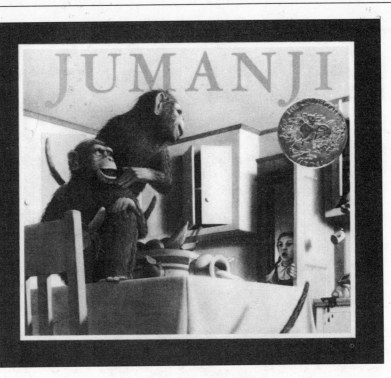

Many critics believe that Chris Van Allsburg is one of the finest illustrators making books today. He works very hard to make his pictures exciting. Chris believes that making a book is a lot like making a movie. The illustrator is like the director—the person who decides where to place the camera. When you look at Chris's illustrations, think about where he

JUST A DREAM
STORY AND PICTURES BY CHRIS VAN ALLSBURG

"I'm pleased when my own drawings are a little mysterious to me. I like to create a world where not everything is possible, but where strange things may happen."

"places the camera" for each scene. Sometimes the camera, or *point of view*, is very close to a character; other times the camera may be up in the clouds, looking down upon a wide landscape. The camera changes position often, making the story dramatic and lively.

Chris explains, "After I have the text and know essentially what has to be illustrated, I'll do a lot of crude thumbnail sketches which deal with point of view."

"The truth is, there are many ways to do an illustration. In terms of point of view and lighting alone, there are an infinite number of possibilities. Through sketching, I narrow my choices."

DO IT YOURSELF!

Select a picture from one of Chris's books. Think about the different ways you could "move the camera" to show the same scene. For example, if the picture is a close up, think about how it would look if you "pulled the camera back." You'd see a lot more of the surrounding area, but you might lose the emotion on a character's face. Make several rough sketches, using different perspectives of the same scene.

Bernard Waber

SELECTED TITLES

The House on East 88th Street
1962

Just Like Abraham Lincoln
1964

Lyle, Lyle, Crocodile
1965

An Anteater Named Arthur
1967

A Firefly Named Torchy
1970

Ira Sleeps Over
1972

Dear Hildegarde
1980

Bernard
1982

◆

Born:
September 27, 1924, in Philadelphia, Pennsylvania

Home:
Baldwin Harbor, New York

Perhaps the most important aspect of writing, Bernard Waber believes, is *thinking* about writing.

"A lot of my books begin with ideas that amuse me, but that's just the starting point," Waber explains. "The nice thing about humor is that after you have an idea that you think is humorous, there is always another side that's sad and complicated. Those are the things you discover after you start writing."

The story *Ira Sleeps Over*, for example, began with a simple idea: a boy is torn between the comfort of his teddy bear and his desire to go to a sleepover. But gradually, by writing and thinking about the idea, new dimensions of the story began to emerge for Waber. He says, "If you work hard on something, and think about it very deeply, new ideas sort of bubble to the surface."

That's why revising—which literally means, "to see again"—is so important. While revising, the author is given the opportunity to take a second look at the story. Bernard Waber understands it this way, "I find that while rewriting—even just retyping a page—new things come in that I hadn't thought about before. Rewriting is important. I don't think you are finished after only one or two drafts. Rewriting is not only polishing sentences; it is also a process of searching for new things to improve your story."

Without rewriting, Waber could not have written *Ira Sleeps Over*—one of his best-loved books. Bernard wrote a first version of *Ira Sleeps Over*, which no one, besides his editor, has ever seen. "I sent in an early version to my

publisher," Waber recalls, "I thought I had finished with it. Then an entirely different writing style just suddenly popped into my head. I rewrote the story entirely. Then I got a call from my editor. She said that she pretty much liked the first version. But I said, 'Well, actually, I have a second version for you.'" The second version was even better. It's the *Ira Sleeps Over* that readers know and love.

THE YOUNGEST IN THE FAMILY

Bernard Waber grew up in a household with two older brothers and an older sister. He reflects, "It's taken me a long time to realize the richness I had. Nowadays, I finally understand how much I got from my siblings. They were very artistic. I had a brother who loved literature and chess; I suppose he passed that on to me. I had another brother who liked to write and draw. My sister played piano. She even wrote love letters for her friends, like Cyrano de Bergerac!"

As the youngest in a creative family, Bernard found plenty of time to daydream. "I lived a fantasy life," he said. Part of that fantasy life involved going to the movies and staying all day long. He would sit in the theater and watch the same movie over and over again, until one of his parents finally arrived to drag him home.

Like many artists who both write and illustrate, Waber finds that his dual roles make him feel slightly schizophrenic. "When I am writing, I think of myself as a writer. But when I am illustrating, I think of myself as an illustrator. I think, though, that I try to create

Lyle, Lyle, Crocodile
by BERNARD WABER

"You want to write from the heart, that's the important thing."

situations with my writing that will be fun to illustrate. The writer in me tries to please the illustrator."

Almost all writers aspire to give up their "regular" jobs to become full-time writers. But not Bernard Waber. He liked his regular job too much. (Until recently, Waber worked as a graphic designer on *Life* and *People* magazines.) Waber thinks that having a full-time job actually may have helped his writing: "Having another job gave me artistic freedom; I didn't have to worry about making money through my books. I was able to write whatever I wanted to."

Bernard Waber enjoys visiting children in schools across the country. The part he enjoys most, he says, is talking with fellow writers. "These days, with so many children writing their own stories, it's interesting to talk to them about writing. They ask thoughtful questions about where ideas come from and the various stages of writing. I'm very impressed with their knowledge."

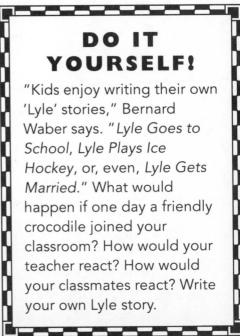

DO IT YOURSELF!

"Kids enjoy writing their own 'Lyle' stories," Bernard Waber says. "*Lyle Goes to School, Lyle Plays Ice Hockey*, or, even, *Lyle Gets Married*." What would happen if one day a friendly crocodile joined your classroom? How would your teacher react? How would your classmates react? Write your own Lyle story.

Vera B. Williams

SELECTED TITLES

◆

Born:
January 28, 1927, in Hollywood,
California

Home:
New York, New York

❝**I** like to visit schools, because I really like hanging around with children," says Vera Williams.

When Vera visits a classroom, she tries to help children understand how a book is made. She says, "I try to turn the whole thing into an example of what I do. Sometimes when I visit, I put tape over my mouth and don't speak at all. I just start to draw. Then I take the tape off my mouth and say, 'Well, that's me as an illustrator—drawing is one way of talking.' And if I make mistakes, which of course I do, I get the children to play editor. I say, 'Well, you see, I don't hand it to you perfect!' "

Vera enjoys children because they give her the chance to be playful. She also enjoys the questions kids ask. She says, "They ask things like, 'Do you have a limousine?' or 'How come you're so old?'" Vera laughs, "That's easy to answer—I was born in 1927!"

When illustrating in front of children, Vera often likes to examine what makes a face seem more like a girl's or a boy's. She says, "I'd draw this face. At first, I'd just draw this empty thing. Sometimes I'd joke: 'Is it a boy or a girl?' They'd yell 'Boy!' or 'Girl!' Meanwhile, there's no features at all. So I'd say, 'Don't be silly, it's a potato!' "

What has Vera learned from her experiments? "Short hair always makes it a boy," she says, "even when there are girls in the classroom with short haircuts. Heart-shaped faces are thought to be female, while long, square faces are male. It's very complicated.

"For instance, as soon as I put eyelashes on a drawing they all yell, 'It's a girl!' Then I have to ask them if boys come without eyelashes. This always ends in a lot of laughter and, I trust, some new thoughts."

Growing up, Vera and her older sister, Naomi, were encouraged to express their creative talents. On Saturdays, they traveled together on the subway to attend art classes. In high school, Vera wrote and illustrated her first book, which was about a gigantic banana.

The emotions and experiences of childhood continue to play an important role in Vera's work. "When I first started doing my books for children, I tried to remember the pictures from my own childhood, how I did them, what I was feeling when I made them."

Vera confides, "Many of my illustrations appear to have been dashed off—and so they were, some of them over and over. Sometimes I select one entire drawing from a number of attempts; sometimes I cut and paste parts from various drawings."

Because Vera does so much revision, she admits, "I don't have such good work habits when it comes to getting things done quickly. I am not content with my first, second, or third solutions. I do incredible numbers of sketches. I just have to draw and draw and draw until I get it right."

WRITING ON POSTCARDS

Usually, Vera begins the creative process by thinking about and writing down the story. The illustrations come later. But that wasn't the case with *Stringbean's Trip to the Shining Sea*. For that book, Vera says, "I never really wrote a story."

"No typed manuscript exists for that book—I wrote it on postcards, because the book has a postcard style," Vera says. "So it wasn't written and then translated

to postcards, it actually consists of postcards that I made up as I went along. I tried to work in such a way that the process and the outcome would be one."

Writing on postcards, Vera Williams noticed, was very different from regular writing. She explains, "On postcards, we tend to drop off the subject of the sentence. Ordinarily you'd say, 'I went to the Grand Canyon yesterday.' But a lot of postcards start, 'Went to Grand Canyon.' You do absolutely anything to save space."

> **"I've always had the feeling— even from childhood—that lettering, text, and pictures are very closely related."**

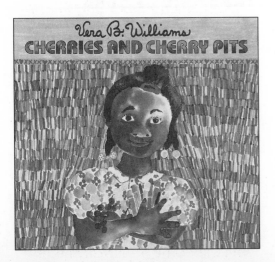

DO IT YOURSELF!

Try, as Vera Williams did, to tell a story by writing a series of postcards. Get some blank index cards. Draw pictures on one side and write on the other. Create a story about a trip to a strange, new land.

Jane Yolen

SELECTED TITLES

The Emperor and the Kite
1967

The Girl Who Loved the Wind
1972

The Girl Who Cried Flowers and Other Tales
1974

Dream Weaver
1979

Commander Toad in Space
1980

Sleeping Ugly
1981

Owl Moon
(Caldecott Medal)
1987

The Devil's Arithmetic
1988

◆

Born:
February 11, 1939, in New York, New York

Home:
Hatfield, Massachusetts

Readers frequently ask Jane Yolen, "Where do you get your great ideas?" But there really isn't a satisfactory answer to that question because most authors don't honestly know where their ideas come from. For that reason, perhaps it's better to ask, "What do you do with your ideas once you get them?" Now, that's a question that Jane Yolen can answer.

"I keep an idea file," she says. "I always scribble down ideas when I get them. I find that so many ideas come to me that if I don't write them down, they're gone.

"I have one whole file-cabinet drawer filled with file folders that have maybe a paragraph, two paragraphs, or a page or two of this new idea. Whenever I've reached a point with my other work—that either nothing's going well or I've finished some major project—I go and look through all those files to see if there's anything that says, Me! It's my turn, I'm ready. I want to be the next story."

But ideas don't become books overnight. It's a gradual process that sometimes takes several years. Jane offers an example: "I had been writing poems about cats, not knowing what to do with them. I was thinking maybe, eventually, I'd have a book of cat poems. But something was not there. I had been writing these poems for maybe eight years. And then one day, the phrase 'raining cats and dogs' came to me. And I said, I'm going to write a book of cats *and* dogs. It's going to be called, *Raining Cats and Dogs*. With that incentive, I wrote some dog poems to match the cat poems. So you see, that's an idea that moved along over many years."

THE SOUND OF WORDS

As a writer, Jane is drawn to magical or mythological subjects. Strange events occur in her stories: a girl cries flowers, a boy learns how to fly, a deer turns into a unicorn. In Jane's hands, even a realistic story such as *Owl Moon* conveys a mood of magic, mystery, and moonlight.

Perhaps the biggest influence on Yolen's writing is the oral tradition of storytellers. The sound of the words is very important to her. "I read everything out loud. So I think, instead of seeing pictures, I am hearing the story as music." She believes that it is important for young writers to try to write every day. It's also important to realize that every writer gets rejections. Even writers with more than 110 books, like Jane Yolen.

"I got one last week," Jane admits. "That's fine. Because a rejection doesn't mean that you're no good, and it doesn't necessarily mean that the piece is no good. It means that one person didn't like it. One person. My way of dealing with rejections is to get angry for about a minute and a half and then to send the manuscript out again."

Yolen also spends a good part of her time speaking out against censorship. Censorship stems from the word *censure*, which means to criticize severely. When books are censored, they are kept out of classrooms and libraries. For example, some people believe that children should not be allowed to read books or see

> "I've always felt that the audience I'm writing for is myself—the child that I was and the child who is still inside me."

movies that have witches in them. Jane Yolen disagrees: "To say that you can't have children see *The Wizard of Oz* because there are witches in it is absolutely ridiculous."

Yolen believes that many people who favor censorship misunderstand literature. "I think that the people who are most involved in censorship—especially of fantasy books—have no sense of metaphor. If you don't have a sense of metaphor, then you begin to believe these things are absolutely point-for-point true, in the small sense, the lowercase *t*.

"I think fantasy books and metaphor teach us about Truth with a capital *T*. They are talking about love, honor, loyalty, and bravery—not about witchcraft!"

Jane Yolen offers this advice to aspiring writers: "It's important to keep open your sense of wonder, your sense of curiosity, your sense of exploration. I think good writers have to be in touch with that openness—that willingness to be surprised."

OWL MOON
by Jane Yolen
illustrated by John Schoenherr

DO IT YOURSELF!

Jane Yolen sometimes invents stories by beginning with a situation and asking herself, What next? Try it yourself. The situation can be anything. A cow falls in love with a frog or a spaceship lands in your backyard. Ask yourself, What happens next? The answer you come up with is the story you should be writing!

Ed Young

SELECTED TITLES

◆

Born:
November 28, 1931, in Tientsin, China

Home:
Hastings-on-Hudson, New York

C aldecott Medal-winning illustrator Ed Young doesn't like to overemphasize the *process* of creativity. He says, "To me, it is the attitude behind everything that is more important than the procedure."

A deeply thoughtful man, Ed Young believes that the creation of art involves much more than technical skill. Drawing and writing, he says, "are expressions of the inner rather than the outer person."

In practicing the art of calligraphy, Young learned to refine his brush strokes as well as to achieve a greater sensitivity to his craft. In calligraphy, as in life, Young believes that attitude is of prime importance. "A person has to know the nature of a brush, the nature of ink in the brush, the nature of ink applied by the brush onto paper. That person has to be friends with all of these in order to see what the brush is capable of doing.

"It is like training a horse. A person has to know what the nature of the horse is in order to ride it correctly. If the horse knows that the person understands him and gives him every possibility of exploring his potential, the horse will be very happy. And so with the brush."

EXPLORING WITH A PENCIL

Once he has selected a manuscript, Young immediately begins by making a series of sketches. The process is similar to an exploration; with each sketch, Young searches for the proper tone and image for the story. He says, "First I do little thumbnails right on the margin of the manuscript whenever there is a picture that comes to me. I just scribble, and the pictures that I draw are no more than maybe a half or three-quarters of an inch. It's just a record of images that are in my head."

In what he calls rounds, Young revisits his initial sketches and expands upon them. Slowly, he adds more and more details, and the tiny pictures grow larger. Young explains, "They graduate, let's say, from the first set of very small thumbnails to something two or three inches tall by five or six inches wide. At that point, I start to go into the characters or buildings or costumes, that kind of thing."

During the next round, the element of research becomes very important. In the first sketches, Young only sought to capture a general impression, a feeling. Now he seeks painstaking accuracy. The pictures themselves seem to ask him these questions: In what style should the characters be dressed? What are the trees and flowers like in that part of the world? What is the style of architecture?

To achieve this level of accuracy, Young turns to magazines, books, libraries, museums, or wherever he can find the information he needs. Young goes to all the trouble because he feels that factual detail helps create a believable fantasy. As an artist, he is preparing an imaginative world for the reader to visit. The trees, the flowers, the buildings—everything—must be true to that world.

An example of Young's emphasis on detail can be found in the work he did for *Lon Po Po*. The story, which is a Chinese version of "Little Red Riding Hood," involves a wolf and children. (Lon Po Po means "Granny Wolf" in Chinese.) Ed Young explains how he made the wolf and children believable. "I drew a whole series on how wolves communicate with each other, using their ears, their tails, and the way they hold themselves. That had to be right because the wolf talks to the children in the story, so he has to be alive to them. Then I had to know how the children talked to each other, how they lived in the compound, how the trees would grow. Once you know everything about

the story, you can express it in fresh ways."

Ed Young was born in China, grew up in Shanghai, and later moved to Hong Kong before eventually settling in the United States. Of his childhood, Young recalls: "Our summer nights were usually spent on the flat roof of the three-story house that my father designed. Against the background of crickets chirping in the starry night, my father would spin endless tales of his own to entertain our imagination until the heat finally subsided. I have never forgotten the images I saw in my mind as I listened."

> "I have never lost the child in me. I think everyone has a child in him that responds to anything that has true meaning."

DO IT YOURSELF!

Ed Young thinks kids who like to draw should make up their own illustrations to go with their favorite stories. Why not try it? Your own pictures will help you tell the story the way *you* see it. "There are things," he says, "that pictures can do that words never can."

INTERMEDIATE BOOKS

AUTHORS AND ILLUSTRATORS

The Wart found . . . that he had tumbled off the drawbridge, landing with a smack on his side in the water. He found that the moat and the bridge had grown hundreds of times bigger. He knew that he was turning into a fish.

"Oh, Merlyn," cried the Wart. "Please come too."

"Just for this once," said a large and solemn tench beside his ear, "I will come. But in the future you will have to go by yourself. Education is experience, and the essence of experience is self-reliance."

T. H. WHITE, *The Once and Future King*
published by PUTNAM
© 1958 by T. H. WHITE

Like Merlyn, writers who create timeless works for children are magicians. In their imaginations they conjure worlds, and using tools as simple as paper, pencil, pen, and keyboard, they transform their inner visions into unforgettable books, shared with millions of readers. Like their ancient predecessor, these conjurers are teachers as well. They use their storytelling powers to offer lessons about truth, life, death, friendship, love, hate, courage, and despair.

Though Merlyn did not accompany the Wart on most of his adventures in *The Once and Future King*, he did go along "just once." Although we usually read wonderful books without a chance to get to know the authors, you are about to meet this special group of Merlyns "just once." The thirty legendary authors profiled in this half of the book will tell you about their childhoods, their moments of triumph and despair, their sources of inspiration, and their individual writing processes. Here and there you will get a glimmer of insight into ways these artists make their magic. Nobody can truly teach another person how to write, but these authors certainly offer hints: Listen to your inner voice. Write about what you know. Write about what you *don't* know. Tell the truth. And, above all, stick with it.

I hope you enjoy meeting these remarkable people as much as I did, and that you join me in thanking them for their willingness to share themselves with us—their fans, their supporters, and their students.

DEBORAH KOVACS

Joan Aiken

SELECTED TITLES

◆

Born:
September 4, 1924, in Sussex, England

Home:
Sussex, England, and New York, New York

Since she was five years old, Joan Aiken has carried a small notebook with her wherever she goes. When she visits a classroom of children and they ask her where she gets her ideas, Joan pulls out her current 2-by 5-inch notebook and reads aloud some of the entries, such as: "Sign: Danger. . . . Keep clear of unpropped body. . . . Road Sign: Slow—Toads Crossing. . . . Bottles on roof of Turkish house indicate marriagable girl inside. . . . Parrot on bridge of ship. . . . Lady rents hats. . . . Degrees in Prophecy. . . . Graveyard like chessboard. . . . Tightrope walker on vapour-trail. . . . Rats on board plane."

"I show children the notebook I have filled with all of my jottings," Joan continues, "and try to convince them to start keeping a notebook of their own."

CLIPPINGS, PICTURES, AND IDEAS

When Joan sets out to write a book, the process is gradual. Her ideas generally come from one focal situation, which over a period of months grows into a plot. For example, *The Shadow Guests* came from the experience of a godchild whose invented friends had started to become threatening and overbearing. *The Cuckoo Tree* came from the idea of a long-awaited reunion that is instantly impinged upon and broken up.

Joan says, "These nuclear ideas rapidly begin to accumulate a kind of coral reef of characters and developments and situations." Once she begins a novel, she keeps a folder for it where she puts everything relevant that she comes across, such as newspaper clippings, pictures, and ideas.

Before writing a book, Joan takes a lot of notes. If possible, she goes to the locale of the book and stays there. These days, she is writing a book with a nineteenth-century Industrial Revolution background. To prepare, she has taken a trip down a coal mine, studied early iron-smelting techniques, and early printing presses.

Joan is a solitary creator. She admits, "It's quite out of the question for me to write when there is someone else in the same room. Even if he or she is under a Trappist vow—just the vibrations of another personality are too distracting to allow me to write."

When Joan finds her mind

blocked, she takes a three-mile walk to clear her head, "which it sometimes does." She says, "On the whole, I find it is best to keep urging my mind at a problem." If a block is really serious, she may take a break for a week or a month and do something else. "But I never like breaking off," she says. "I always feel that a book has more strength and homogeneity if the first draft, at least, was all done under one impulse. I find that writing is a self-generating activity—the more one does it, the more easily it flows. And vice versa. The first few pages after a long gap are always very sticky and have to be rewritten many times."

Joan is a visual writer. Her pictures are "first of the characters, then of the locations." Sometimes she makes maps. "Whether the places in stories are real or my own invention, I always know exactly what they look like."

"Keep a notebook," is the advice Joan Aiken grants aspiring writers. "Try to write a few pages every day. Never write anything that bores you. Collect interesting stories from newspapers. Think of the end of a story before you start it. Read as much as you possibly can—reading is an essential occupation for any would-be writer."

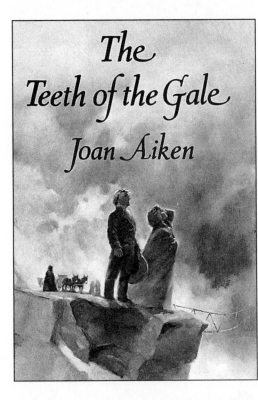

"I've read a lot to my own children, including my own books in installments as I wrote them. Their criticisms were very useful."

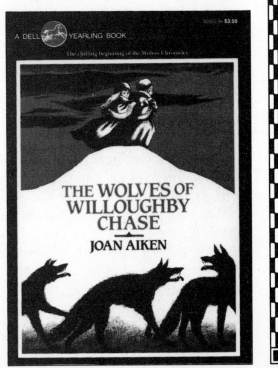

DO IT YOURSELF!

Here is a writing activity from Joan Aiken: "Chop a couple dozen news stories out of a week's daily papers. Shuffle them around and try to compose a story out of any three or four. Do the same thing with remarks that you overhear in the street or with classified newspaper advertisements. Imagine someone you know well in some fearful predicament; how would he extricate himself?"

Lloyd Alexander

SELECTED TITLES

Born:
January 30, 1924, in Philadelphia, Pennsylvania

Home:
Drexel Hill, Pennsylvania

Sometimes as Lloyd Alexander writes, he feels his body move as his character's would. He relishes this state, and says of it, "I'm able for a brief period to get into that marvelous place called *the zone*. Athletes and musicians know it. It's a moment that doesn't last too long, a moment of very relaxed intense concentration. A basketball player in the zone feels as though everything around him slows down. He says, 'Now I'm going to drop that ball in the basket,' and just rises up to do it."

When Lloyd is writing, he imagines he's sitting in a movie theater watching the movie of what he wants to write. "Sometimes the vision is not clear," he explains. "If you can see what you're doing, it sure helps."

Says Lloyd, "There are only two sources that any writer could have—what you observe and how you interpret it. My own personality influences me, and what's important to me influences me. That mixture is where the ideas come from."

AN OLD MANUAL TYPEWRITER

He writes on an old manual typewriter. "Someday it's going to break and I'm going to be crumbled. But I bought its twin and I have it put away, so I've got a backup." He writes a lot of notes before he starts typing a first draft. He rewrites a great deal. "I guess I've written individual pages maybe thirty times—chapters, certainly five times." He's rewritten some of his books as many as three times.

Why does he rewrite so much? "Somehow, after I read what I've written, I see that I could do it better. I see I could improve my language or my pacing. I get an insight into what I'm trying to do that I didn't have before. Unfortunately, you learn from your mistakes. Unless you're a genius, I don't see how you could do it right the first time."

When Lloyd gets writer's block, which happens to him often, it's very painful. "I've read books on the subject, trying to figure out the answer. But there is only one answer: force yourself to write, no matter how bad it is. That is the hard part." To shake off a block, Lloyd advises writers to try to be "as loose and spontaneous as possible, to fix it up later."

Lloyd Alexander enjoys reading just about anything. He taught himself how to read when he was just three years old. "I grabbed hold of my parents' books by accident and didn't let go," he recalls. Lloyd wasn't the stereotypical bookworm though. "I don't want to give the impression I was a pale, wan, frail little boy sitting in a corner," he says. "I played, I had friends, I knocked around."

Although Lloyd relishes the activity, he's not doing too much reading these days. "When I'm actively working, I try not to read very much, or at least nothing very good, because it will change my feelings in some way. I don't want to lose my mental balance. I'm focusing on a certain state or feeling and a good book will mess it up."

In his spare time, Lloyd loves

to play the violin. Every Monday morning he gets together with a group of friends and plays chamber music. Lloyd also likes to talk with children. He says, "I have a great time talking with kids, which is strange because I'm very shy."

Lloyd Alexander has this advice for kids who like to write: "Read as much as you can. Write as much as you can. Be as alive as you can. Be patient. Everything beyond that is detail. If you quit, the game's over. If you persist, you still have a chance."

> "I would hope, as kids grow up, they'll one way or another find my books. I hope, if they find them at the right time, that they'll read them and like them."

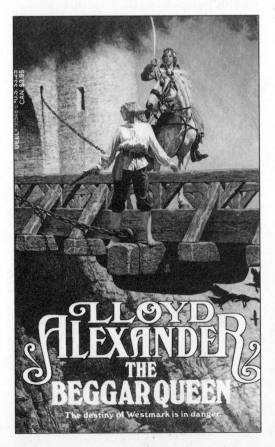

DO IT YOURSELF!

Here's a writing activity from Lloyd Alexander: "Write a letter. If you want to tell a story and you don't know how to begin and you're flopping around and don't know what to do and it's all vague, put it in the form of a letter. Write a letter to Shakespeare if you want. 'Dear Bill, I'm working on a story, and I'm trying to . . .' All of a sudden, before you know what you're doing, you're into the story."

William H. Armstrong

SELECTED TITLES

Sounder
(Newbery Medal)
1970

Sour Land
1971

**Through Troubled Waters:
A Young Father's Struggle
with Grief**
1983

◆

Born:
September 14, 1914, in Lexington, Virginia

Home:
Kent, Connecticut

One moonlit October night more than twenty years ago, William Armstrong took a walk. He heard the call of an owl, which reminded him of another sound he had once heard about in a story he was told as a young boy. That sound was the bay of the coon dog Sounder. The teller of the tale was an older black man, who worked as a schoolteacher in the winter and a handyman in the summer. On that October night, as he heard the echo of the owl's call across the Housatonic River valley, Armstrong realized it was his duty to share the story of Sounder.

ALWAYS THREE QUESTIONS

He is proud of *Sounder* and of the effect it has had on generations of children. "I get hundreds of letters because *Sounder* is read by practically every sixth grader," says Armstrong. "In these letters, they always ask the same three questions. The first question is, What happened to the boy? I tell them to read *Sour Land*, which is the sequel to *Sounder*."

The second question is, Why don't the people in the book have names? Armstrong answers that he wanted the story to stand for thousands of people, not just a few. "If I'd given each of the characters a name, then the story would be about only one family. Since I didn't name them, they stand for all families, black and white, who have to struggle in the world but through love and self-respect and a desire to improve, win."

The third question is, Why does the book have such a sad ending? To that, Armstrong responds that the book has a happy ending. "What are the most important things that we hold onto as we walk through the earth? The most important things are good memories. And what did the boy remember about his life? Did he remember his father, crippled, dragging half his body home from the stone quarry? Did he remember Sounder, mutilated by the deputy sheriff's shotgun? Did he remember the lonely agony of the silence that comes with sorrow? No, no! Read the last paragraph of the story: 'Years later, walking the earth as a man, it would all sweep back over him, again and again, like an echo of the wind. The pine trees would look down forever on a lantern burning out of oil but not going out. A harvest moon would cast shadows forever of a man walking upright, his dog bouncing after him. And the quiet of the night would fill and echo again with the deep voice of Sounder, the great coon dog.'

"That's what you remember," says Armstrong. "If we remember the bitter things, we go through the earth hating everything and everybody, gnawing away at our own souls like trapped animals. The book has a happy ending, but they've missed it."

Armstrong never set out to be a novelist. His greatest interest has been in studying and teaching history. Every day, Armstrong still rides his bicycle the mile between the hillside home he built for himself and the Kent School, where he has taught history for almost fifty years.

He says, "I really hate to write, so what I do is live with an idea for a long, long time. When I'm outside splitting wood or cleaning out the sheep barn, I'm thinking

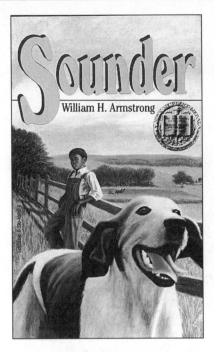

> "My favorite part of writing is going down to the basement to sharpen my pencil."

about it and going over what happened or what's going to happen. When I'm ready to write, I write with a pencil on a lined tablet, just the way you do in the third grade. I always advise people to write with a pencil rather than a word processor, because with a pencil you can feel the words. I tell them to write with a pencil that writes dark. There it is, you meant it, you've borne down on it."

He writes in a room that overlooks the Housatonic River valley. Five miles in the distance, he can see mountains. "My window is eight feet wide. My desk is two great two-inch-thick boards put together, thirty inches wide and eight feet long."

When he writes he feels as if he is part of the story. "I love the mother in *Sounder* so much that when I was writing the book, if I was out splitting wood or doing something that took heavy breathing, I couldn't even think about her because I would get a lump in my throat."

Asked his advice to children who like to write, William Armstrong replies: "Number one: Read, read, read, and keep on reading. Number two: Listen to your teachers. Number three: Be proud of your written work. Dot the *i*'s and cross the *t*'s. Neatness grows from dotted *i*'s and crossed *t*'s into beautiful pages."

DO IT YOURSELF!

William Armstrong suggests that children try this writing activity: "Think about what you want to be when you grow up. Find somebody in your town or city who has that job. Go interview that person. Then write a page or two about what they do. Is the job all you expected it to be?"

Judy Blume

SELECTED TITLES

Born:
February 12, 1938, in Elizabeth, New Jersey

Home:
New York, New York

T hough Judy was a happy child, like most children, she had a dark side. When she was around nine or ten, she thought she was responsible for the well-being of her family. "I believed that unless I said ritualistic prayers five times every day something terrible would happen," she says. The secret to her extraordinary ability to write for children may be that she still remembers what that dark side was like.

"There's reassurance in finding out that what you do and think aren't weird at all, but that they're okay," she says.

Judy Blume feels very good when she receives a letter from a reader who says, "I talk to God just like Margaret in *Are You There, God? It's Me, Margaret* does. But I always thought I was the only one."

TIME TO DREAM

When Judy was a child, although she liked playing with the other kids in the neighborhood, her inner, secret life was very important to her. "I was very lucky that my mother allowed me to have plenty of time alone. I think kids today rush from activity to activity. When do they have the time to dream or play by themselves or just think? I don't know what happens when you don't have time to dream and think and play."

Judy writes at home in a sunny room with a wonderful view of New York City from one window and the Hudson River from another. She does most of her writing in the morning. Whenever she starts a book, she fills a notebook with details about characters, including scraps of dialogue and things she doesn't want to forget. "I continue to take notes throughout the entire first draft. By the end of the first draft, I usually know my characters pretty well."

Once her first draft is complete, she begins rewriting immediately. "I'm a rewriter," she says. "That's the part I like best. I despise and am terrified by a first draft. But once I have a pile of paper to work with, it's like having the pieces of a puzzle. I just have to put the pieces together to make a picture." Most of her books take her more than a year to write, though her most recent, *Fudge-a-Mania*, went more quickly.

As Judy writes, she listens. "I have an ear for dialogue," she says. "I hear it inside my head." Her son is a filmmaker. He has taught her a lot about being able to visualize as well. "I find now that I can run scenes though my mind like a movie."

Judy Blume has the following advice for young people who want to become writers: "Don't be in a hurry to be published. Be professional first. Learn to imitate other people's styles. Eventually you'll come up with your own voice. You have to write what you really,

really care about. If it's not real to you, it's not going to be real to your readers. You have to watch and listen." Above all, Judy believes that writers should not be afraid to read their work out loud. "When you read aloud, you can hear what doesn't work."

Writing out loud helps those who don't like to write, Judy

Blume thinks. Her son found writing to be a real chore, even though he was very verbal. Judy would sit at the typewriter and say to him, "Say it to me." She'd type his words and then show it to him and say, "You did it. You wrote the paper!"

"I get my best ideas scribbling with a pencil."

DO IT YOURSELF!

When Judy Blume was in the sixth grade, she had to write book reports—lots of book reports. To amuse herself, sometimes she would make up book reports based on imaginary books. "I'd make up the title, author, plot, characters, the whole thing. I never got caught." Write your own book report on an imaginary book. If you're feeling really ambitious, write the book too!

Betsy Byars

SELECTED TITLES

Born:
August 7, 1928, in Charlotte, North Carolina

Home:
Clemson, South Carolina

Betsy Byars thinks of her novels as scrapbooks of her life. "What do people who don't write do with these details?" she wonders. "When I see something quirky or real or interesting, I put it in a book."

When Betsy gets an idea for a book, she writes it down immediately. "Even if I only get the title," she says, "I write the title down." If she's in the middle of writing another book, she breaks away from it for a few minutes and writes down the new idea, just to get it started. "I find I have a lot of creative energy at the beginning of a new project," she explains. "I don't want to lose that energy."

Sometimes ideas for a book come to her out of order. If she's writing Chapter Two of a book and gets an idea for Chapter Seven, she writes, "Chapter Seven," then she writes her idea. "An idea is fleeting," she says. "It's easier to put it down as if it were a chapter.

"I work on a word processor for the first draft, but for revisions, I always print out a copy of the book and do my corrections by hand," says Betsy. She usually starts by writing the middle portion of a chapter, which takes up about half a page. Then, when she does her revisions, she goes back and adds the beginning and the end of the chapter.

A LITTLE LOG CABIN

Betsy writes in a little log cabin, which is a ten-minute walk or a five-minute drive from her home. The room she writes in is small—about eight feet by ten feet. "Some people say it makes them claustrophobic, but I like it," she says. "There are lots of things on the walls: posters, letters, pictures from kids. I did knock out one wall and put in a big stained-glass window that I had made. It has all of my favorite flowers in it." But she admits that her surroundings don't matter to her very much. "When I start writing, I'm not very aware of where I am."

Writer's block is not much of a problem for Betsy. Still, there are days when she gets stuck. "If I come to the end of the chapter and I can't think of what to do, I go to the library and pull books off the shelf. I read the first sentence of every chapter. I might go through ten or twenty different books. Finally, I'll find something inspiring, like: 'The telephone rang.' This has never failed me when I'm trying to start a chapter."

As a child, Betsy read a great deal. But she never thought of herself as a writer. She changed her mind when she was a young mother at home with her four kids. In those days, she used to read *The Saturday Evening Post*. At the back of the magazine there was a page called Postscript. "It was full of funny things that people sent in. I used to read it and say to myself, I could do that. That is not so hard. That's how I got started. I wrote a Postscript and sent it in to *The Saturday Evening Post*. They accepted it and paid me $75. That was good for my confidence—to make a sale the very first time I tried."

To her readers who want to be writers, she says, "When I was in school, the teachers always told me, 'Write about what you know.' I always thought, That's the stupidest thing I've ever heard. You've got to make up stuff!

> "I used to think that writers were like wells, and sooner or later we'd use up what had happened to us. I imagine we would if it weren't for that elusive quality—creativity."

"But the truth is, the words *author* and *authority* go together. When you write about what you know, you write with authority. Authority is the greatest gift a writer can have."

Betsy Byars knows that there are some kids who don't like to write. To them, she suggests: "If you're not good at writing, find out what you are good at. But try to keep writing too. I feel that everybody ought to be able to express themselves in words on the written page. You're going to have to do this your whole life. I try to encourage writing as a necessary skill, not just for people who want to be writers, but for everybody."

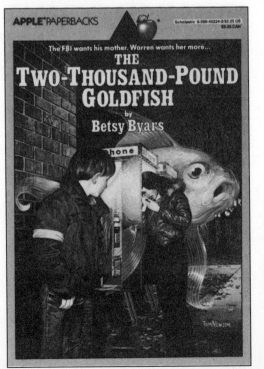

DO IT YOURSELF!

Here is a writing activity from Betsy Byars: "One of my favorite things to give a character is a memory of mine. In *Cracker Jackson* I gave one of the characters my earliest memory of my father. I'd like to see kids try to write down their earliest memories."

Beverly Cleary

SELECTED TITLES

Henry Huggins
1950

Henry and Beezus
1952

Henry and Ribsy
1954

Beezus and Ramona
1955

Fifteen
1956

Henry and the Clubhouse
1962

The Mouse and the Motorcycle
1965

Runaway Ralph
1970

Ramona the Brave
1975

Dear Mr. Henshaw
(Newbery Medal)
1984

Ramona, Forever
1984

The Growing-up Feet
1987

◆

Born:
April 12, 1916, in McMinnville, Oregon
Home:
Northern California coast

Beverly Cleary says she gets her ideas the same way everybody else does: "from experience, from imagination, and from the world around me." The one place she never finds ideas is in other people's books. "I get upset by the number of children who think it's perfectly all right to steal anything from a book."

Beverly says her mind is "a scrap bag of ideas collected over the years." She keeps a composition book with one or two pages dedicated to each book idea. "I sometimes jot down a word or two for something that might fit in the book. Sometimes, I can't remember what the words mean."

Beverly never outlines. She writes with a Pilot Rolling Ball pen on a yellow legal pad. Then she types the story before revising. She says, "By the time I finish my first draft, I've written between the lines and around the edges and on the back of the paper. It's a mess."

A HALF-DOZEN REVISIONS

"Some parts I revise half a dozen times," Beverly says. "Some parts I don't revise at all. I cut a lot. Then I retype the manuscript so it's more legible." She sets the story aside for a couple of weeks so she can look at it with fresh eyes. "I'm tired when I finish a book," she says. "I need a vacation so I can look at it objectively." Before she sends it to her publisher, she has a typist make one last completely clean version.

Beverly writes at a desk in the corner of her bedroom. "Behind is a case with all my books in all editions, including fourteen foreign languages. In front of me is a

painting of a woman sitting at a desk with her garden behind her. It's a painting of a friend by a friend. The title is *Creative Woman*," says Beverly.

When she can't think of what will happen next in the story, she writes something else and returns to her story later. "I do not believe in writer's block," she says. "Creative people are always creative. But that does not mean they can create on demand."

Until Beverly was six years old, she was very much like Ramona Quimby. "I lived on a farm and could be wild and free," she recalls. But once she started school, things changed. "I quickly turned into Ellen Tebbits," she says. "Going to school after living on a farm was a very frightening experience. I learned to be very quiet and to observe. I had to learn how I was supposed to act."

Beverly had a little trouble learning how to read. But once she learned, "I read any story I could get my hands on." She read the entire fairy-tale section of her local library, which was a home away from home. Except for school assignments, she did not write as a child. "I always thought I'd like to write someday, but I didn't do anything about it," she remembers.

Beverly has the following suggestions for would-be professional writers: "If you're serious about becoming a professional writer, prepare to have some other way of earning a living. Many fine writers don't earn enough to live on. Read widely. Master the tools of writing. I know that spelling, punctua-

> ## "I write about people, not problems."

tion, and grammar are boring, but they are necessary."

What does Beverly do when she's not writing? In her spare time, she likes to read. She also enjoys walking and doing handicrafts—both of these activities free her mind so that her imagination can light on new ideas.

DO IT YOURSELF!

Beverly Cleary writes all of her book ideas down in a notebook. Follow her example and start your own story-idea notebook. When you get an idea for a story—a pig that yearns to fly, a girl obsessed with doing cartwheels, a grumpy grandfather—write it down. Remember, the idea doesn't have to be a big one or a finished one—just one that you're fond of and that you want to develop. As you think more about that initial idea, others will no doubt come to you. Write them down too. Over the course of days or weeks, the story will likely come into sharp focus. When it does, the time is ripe to sharpen your pencil and write it.

Roald Dahl

SELECTED TITLES

Born:
September 13, 1916, in Llandaff, South Wales

Died:
November 23, 1990

Most of Roald Dahl's books were written in a tiny brick hut in an apple orchard about two hundred yards away from his main house in Buckinghamshire, England.

The hut was very untidy inside, which amused Roald, because in his big house he was very orderly. Here is how he described it once: "I see that the floor is littered with dead leaves and dust and bits of paper. Over in one corner, there are a few goat droppings, hard and harmless, left there by our nanny-goat, Alma, who paid me a visit last month. For extra warmth the walls are lined with ill-fitting sheets of polystyrene, yellow with age. And spiders, which I adore, make pretty webs in the corners."
Most often, Roald did not notice

his surroundings when he wrote. He said, "When I am here I see only the paper I am writing on, and my mind is far away with Willy Wonka or James or Mr. Fox . . . or whatever else I am trying to cook up. It is out of focus and whistling in the wind."

It was in this hut that Roald Dahl wrote his many classic stories for children and adults. He wrote slowly, painstakingly. He was awed by writers who could turn out a book every two or three years. It took him at least six. "I can't tell you how slowly I write," he said.

A DIFFICULT JOB

Roald Dahl thought that being a writer was difficult. "The writer has to force himself to work," he once said. "He has to make his own hours, and if he doesn't go to his desk at all there is nobody to scold him. If he is a writer of fiction, he lives in a world of fear. Each new day demands new ideas, and he can never be sure whether he is going to come up with them or not.

"Two hours of writing fiction leaves this particular writer absolutely drained," he wrote. "For those two hours he has been miles away, he has been somewhere else, in a different place with totally different people, and the effort of swimming back into normal surroundings is great. It is almost a shock. The writer walks out of his workroom in a daze."

Roald didn't start out to be a writer at all. In fact, when he was fourteen, his English composition teacher wrote the following on his report card: "I have never met a boy who so persistently writes the exact opposite of what he means. He seems incapable of marshalling thoughts on paper."

But after a stint in the Royal Air Force during World War II, which included a near-fatal plane crash, Roald began to understand that he had stories to tell. His first books were about his experiences in the war. He later wrote many short stories for adults, as well as scripts for television and movies. (He wrote the script for the James Bond movie *You Only Live Twice*.)

When he began to tell bedtime stories to his children, he realized that he might have an ability to write for children too. "I believe that the writer for children must be a jokey sort of a fellow," he said. "He must like simple tricks and jokes and riddles and other childish things. He must be unconventional and inventive."

Roald knew what kids like to read. "They love being spooked," he wrote. "They love suspense. They love action. They love ghosts. They love the finding of treasure. They love chocolates and toys and money. They love magic. They love being made to giggle."

Roald thought that writing for kids was harder than writing for adults. "Children don't have the concentration of adults," he said. "Unless you hold them from the first page, they're going to wander away and watch the telly or do something else. They only read for fun; you've got to hold them."

To Roald, the most important and difficult thing about writing fiction was coming up with a plot. "Good, original plots are hard to come by," he said. "You never

"Had I not had children of my own, I would never have written books for children, nor would I have been capable of doing so."

know when a lovely idea is going to flit suddenly into your mind, but by golly, when it does come along, you grab it with both hands and hang onto it tight. The trick is to write it down at once, otherwise you'll forget it."

Ever since he began to write seriously, he kept a notebook in which he wrote down his ideas. "There are ninety-eight pages in the notebook," he said. "I've counted them. And just about every one of them is filled up on both sides with so-called story ideas. Many are not good. But just about every story and every children's book I have ever written has started out as a little three- or four-line note in this little, much-worn, red-covered volume."

Writing did not come easily to Roald Dahl, who died in 1990. But the life of a writer suited him. He once said, "A person is a fool to become a writer. His only compensation is absolute freedom. He has no master except his own soul, and that, I am sure, is why he does it."

DO IT YOURSELF!

In *James and the Giant Peach*, James roams about inside a giant peach. Imagine you have a magical piece of fruit: a strawberry that can read, a banana that grants you your every wish, a bunch of grapes that can't get along. Think of an adventure that fruit would lead you on and write it down. When you're done, you'll have a delicious story to share.

Paula Danziger

Born:
August 18, 1944, in Washington, D.C.

Home:
New York City and Woodstock, New York

Before Paula Danziger starts writing a new book, she cleans out her closets. "I do it to feel organized and also to avoid what I should be doing," she says. While she gets organized, she thinks about what she is going to write. "I've written one book a year for a long time now. After I finish a book, I take a break and I think and think and don't write." Sometimes ideas come quickly to her, but not always. When she feels a case of writer's block coming on, she takes a bath.

Paula's ideas come from her imagination, from observation, and from experience. "It's a real mixture, sometimes more of one than the other," she says. "For example, a friend of mine has a kid with a nose ring. I've always wondered about nose rings. Like, what happens when people who wear nose rings blow their nose?" So Paula gave Amanda, a character in her book, a nose ring (Amanda also has a shaved head). "In the book, Matthew wonders about all the stuff I wanted to know about—how she blows her nose and how she takes the ring out from the side. . . ."

Paula believes good writers set out to tell the best story they can. For Paula, that means going inside herself and finding something really painful or really funny (often the same thing) that will be useful in the story. "I think my next book is going to be about a kid who can't manage money, because I just paid off six credit cards and ripped up three of them. I should never be allowed in a store that sells rhinestones."

PICTURES IN HER MIND

When she writes, Paula has pictures in her mind. She also has pictures on her refrigerator. "Once I was visiting a school. There was a kid there with a great haircut. It was shorter on one side than on the other, and it was dyed blackish-purple. She was dressed so wonderfully and so oppositely from everyone else in the school. I asked her if I could use her look in a book. She said yes. I took lots of pictures of her and kept them on my refrigerator for a long time. The girl's look eventually ended up in a book."

Paula spends a lot of time in England these days. She's appearing on a British television show

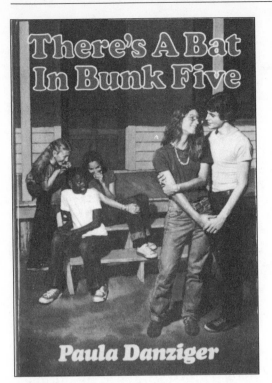

There's A Bat In Bunk Five

Paula Danziger

called "Going Live." "I'm the Book Presenter," she explains. "I'm on the show once a month. I once presented 'Books You Think Will Make You Puke But Won't.'" For that, she went back and reread old classics, like *Little Women*, and told the kids how wonderful they were.

She's having fun with the show, and fun with the kids she's meeting in England. She has always spent lots of her time visiting schools in the United States too. Children like her. "I'm accessible," she says. "I'm honest."

Young people often ask Paula personal questions like, What kind of car do you drive? "They think it's a limo," says Paula. They also ask what her house is like. "I tell them I drive a 1982 Honda and that I've chosen to drive that car because I love it. My house, I tell them, is not posh. It's a wonderful stone house. It looks like elves live in it, like it belongs to fairy-tale characters."

Kids often ask questions that show Paula that her books have

affected them. "They want to know if I've made things up in my books or lived through them. They want to know what happens next after the book ends."

When Paula writes, she really concentrates. "Once I was up in the country working on a book," she says. "I got up in the morning and started working. I didn't even pull up my window shades. At the end of the day, one of my friends called up and said, 'What are you going to do after you finish working?' I said, 'I guess I'll go to the grocery store.' My friend started laughing. 'Have you looked outside today at all?' she asked." Paula lifted the window-shade and looked outside. Three feet of snow had fallen.

Paula understands that some kids don't like to write. "It's all right," she says. "I don't like to cook." It's all right with her, as long as they read. "Hopefully, they'll just read forever."

Sometimes, Paula teaches writing workshops to kids. "Once I taught in the barrios of Los Angeles with a friend." Most of the kids thought they couldn't write or that they hated to write. "We got them to write three sentences in a row, then we said, 'You've done it!' We made it fun, not scary."

Paula has plenty of advice for would-be writers: "Read, write, and trust your instincts. Listen to good criticism, but pick your critics carefully." On her show in England, "Going Live," a girl called up and said, "My teacher says that everything I write is too long. What should I do?" Paula told her to do what her teacher says when she is in school. But, she added, "do it your own way when you're away from school."

> **"My favorite book as a kid was *The Little Engine That Could*. I still go, 'I think I can, I think I can,' when I'm feeling insecure."**

DO IT YOURSELF!

Here is a writing activity from Paula Danziger: "Create a character. First decide whether it's a boy or a girl. What are the character's parents like? What does his or her bedroom closet look like? What is the character's favorite outfit? What does the character want more than anything else (not a material possession)? Give the character a name and a situation. He might learn he has to move; she might be accused of cheating in class. Now write a story about your character."

Barthe DeClements

SELECTED TITLES

Nothing's Fair in Fifth Grade
1981

How Do You Lose Those Ninth Grade Blues?
1983

Sixth Grade Can Really Kill You
1986

Double Trouble
(coauthored by her son, Christopher Greimes)
1987

Five-Finger Discount
1989

Wake Me at Midnight
1991

Breaking Out
1991

◆

Born:
October 8, 1920, in Seattle, Washington

Home:
Snohomish, Washington

For many years, Barthe DeClements worked in schools. First she was a teacher, later a guidance counselor. She got to know kids with problems—big problems. "I was constantly wondering, How is this person put together? How did she evolve? How can she gain autonomy?" says Barthe. She began to write books because she thought they might help children solve some of their problems. "The counseling is still there in my books."

Though she no longer works as a counselor or teacher, she spends as much time in schools as she can. "I still go back to schools whenever I'm going to write a book," she says. "I have lunch with the kids or I teach creative writing to them." When she goes into a school, she takes notes. "I write as fast as I can," says Barthe. "I write down what happens, how they dress, what they say. One sixth-grade class made me a dictionary of slang."

ONE SCENE AT A TIME

Once Barthe finishes researching a book, she writes it one scene at a time. "Sometimes I wake up with scenes in my mind," she says. "On those days, I will stay in bed for a while until the scene forms." She also keeps a notepad beside her bed. "Lots of times a particular scene will occur to me at four in the morning. I write it down so it doesn't escape me."

She works in an upstairs room with windows on three sides overlooking her twenty-two acres of land on the Pilchuk River. "I usually do one scene a day," she says. "I do it while I have energy. When my energy begins to deplete, I quit. I feel that if I don't put energy into a scene, the readers won't feel any impact when they read it. I never write without that energy."

If a scene is very visual, she sees it in her mind as a picture. She even moves her body as her characters do. "If I'm describing a grimace, I make myself grimace. I try to do whatever action I'm describing in the book."

Barthe doesn't fret when she occasionally experiences writer's block. "I don't push it," she says. "It's sort of like learning not to push the river. I give myself time. If you are alone and give yourself time and space, it will work."

After she finishes the first draft of a novel, she begins to rewrite. "I am a compulsive rewriter," she admits. When she is satisfied with her work, she shares it with her children, particularly her son Chris. "He can close his eyes and open his eyes and straighten out a sentence rhythmically when I have it tangled. He can help me make it flow."

When talking to kids about writing, Barthe always tells them how much she rewrites. She encourages them to try to get their work published in magazines such as *Scope, Literary Cavalcade,* and *Stone Soup.* "My own students had stories in these magazines," she says. "They entered contests and won. I think kids sometimes think they cannot do it, but they can."

"Kids don't need books or a special background to become good writers," says Barthe. "It can all come from within themselves. Children tend to think it's impor-

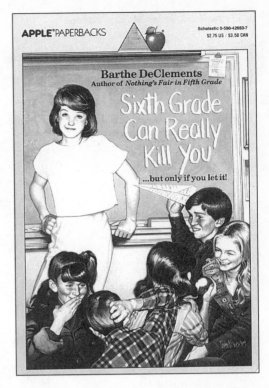

> **"Generally, children want to be good and want to be loved and want to do things that are important to other people. I believe that when children behave badly, it's because they are hurting."**

tant that they write about astronauts or terrible scary things or Hollywood things—something important from far away. I don't agree."

Barthe DeClements thinks that teachers sometimes push children a little too hard when trying to get them to write. "Sometimes teachers say, 'Now get out your pen and paper.' That isn't the way you write," she says. "You must take your time when you write. You must wait until the story bubbles up within you."

DO IT YOURSELF!

Here are two writing activities from Barthe DeClements: Create a dialogue called "Conversation at Midnight." Who do you think would be talking at that hour? What do you think they'd be saying? Write down the conversation that takes place—nothing else. Or, think of a funny, sad, or embarrassing thing that has happened to you—something that you will never forget. Write an essay or a story about that experience.

Eleanor Estes

SELECTED TITLES

The Moffats
1941

The Middle Moffat
1942

Rufus M.
1943

The Sun and the Wind and Mr. Todd
1943

The Hundred Dresses
1944

Ginger Pye
(Newbery Medal)
1951

Pinky Pye
1958

The Alley
1964

The Witch Family
1965

Miranda the Great
1967

The Tunnel of Hugsy Goode
1972

◆

Born:
May 9, 1906, in West Haven, Connecticut

Died:
July 15, 1988

When Eleanor Estes got out of school, she became a children's librarian in New Haven, Connecticut. "I had always wanted to write books," she said, "and I entertained the notion that I could write my own books between stamping out books for the borrowers." This dream was soon shattered. "None of my books were written then," she remembered, "though many of the children whose books I did stamp out have found their way into books I wrote later on.

"I always wanted to become a writer, and I suppose it was because of my long association with children in various public libraries that I unconsciously directed my stories to them—to amuse, to entertain, and to make them laugh or cry."

Memories of her own childhood and of children she knew as an adult formed the basis of Eleanor Estes's writing. "My family life as a child can be sensed from reading most of my books, which drew largely on memories embellished by my wayward imaginings, which took me anywhere." Many times, children asked her, "Are you Janey Moffat?" She would answer, "I don't know. It is very difficult for me to distinguish between what really happened and what I have imagined. I know I and my brothers once rode off with a Salvation Army man in a horse and wagon. And I am not certain whether I walked under a horse or merely entertained the notion."

Eleanor Estes was raised in what was then the rural town of West Haven, Connecticut. Her childhood was very much like that of the children she wrote about in her famous *Moffat* books. "The town had everything a child could want: great vacant fields with daisies and clover and buttercups and an occasional peaceful cow. There were marvelous trees to climb, fishing and clamming in the summertime, ice and snow and sliding down hills in the wintertime."

A STORYTELLING MOTHER

Eleanor may have inherited her writing talent from her mother, who was a good storyteller. "She was very dramatic in her presentation," Eleanor remembers. "We older children had to constantly reassure my younger brother that the giant would not catch Jack and eat him up."

When she wrote, Eleanor tried to work a couple of hours each morning and if possible another hour or so in the afternoon. "Sometimes I am able to follow this schedule," she said. She revised her books over and over, trying to improve them all the way along through to the final proofs. "I feel quite lost when a book is finished and immediately start a new one," she once said.

She usually didn't start enjoying her books until long after they were written. By then, "it's as though someone else had written them, and I laugh at the funny parts," she said. As she wrote, she tried to make each new book as good as it could possibly be, but years might go by before she opened its covers again.

Eleanor liked to be with people, "all kinds and ages and most especially children." She liked to travel. She enjoyed spending time

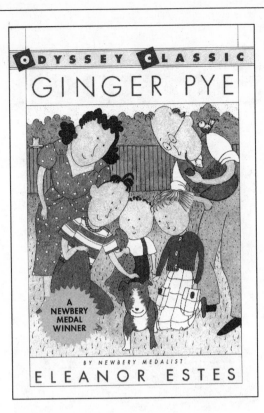

with animals. (Her family always had pets, which showed up in her various books.) She was fond of cooking, though she admitted, "It's possible that I use cooking to put off getting on with my work." She also liked to do nothing, though she had little time for it.

But above all else, Eleanor Estes, who died in 1988, was a children's book writer. She wrote so that her readers could better understand their own lives. "In my writing, I'm holding up a mirror. I hope that what's reflected in it is a true image of childhood and echoes the clear, profound, and unpremeditated thoughts and imageries of childhood."

Eleanor Estes said, "I like to make children laugh or cry, or to move them in some way. I am very happy that my books have been translated into a number of different languages, and I am grateful to the children everywhere who have looked into my mirror and liked what they have seen there."

DO IT YOURSELF!

Ginger Pye is Eleanor Estes's Newbery-winning story about an intellectual dog. It's based on a pet that once lived with her family. Do you know a quirky animal? A cat that loves television? A snobby turtle? If so, write a story about that animal. If not, make one up.

Louise Fitzhugh

SELECTED TITLES

Harriet the Spy
1964

The Long Secret
1965

*Nobody's Family Is Going
to Change*
1974

◆

Born:
October 5, 1928, in Memphis,
Tennessee

Died:
November 19, 1974

Louise Fitzhugh did not set out to be a writer of children's books. Her first great love was painting. "She did some beautiful work," remembers writer Marijane Meaker (M. E. Kerr). "Louise spent a lot of time painting. Painting was her great love. All her paintings are marvelous."

Louise's editor Charlotte Zolotow remembers her paintings too. "They were very strange," she recalls. "Sort of dreamlike, distorted, contorted figures, some with a beautiful sense of color, an uneasy sense of rising color. I remember one that was a pale pastel orange, but with an intensity. It was pale and it wasn't. There was a glow about it."

Louise discovered her writing talent when she collaborated with a friend, Sandra Scoppetone, on a book called *Suzuki Beane*. But her most well-known book was the next one, which she wrote by herself. It's based on a story Marijane Meaker told her about her own childhood.

"I used to have a spy club," says her friend Marijane. "I told her about the spy club. In the club, children were rewarded for the amount of license numbers they could produce. She beat me to the punch by writing it first. But the story she wrote was very Louise."

A LONELY CHILDHOOD

In *Harriet the Spy*, the character of Harriet, her relationship to her parents, and her family life were partly drawn from Louise's own childhood. Her mother abandoned Louise when she was very young to pursue a career as a dancer. As a result, Louise was raised by her father, a well-to-do Memphis lawyer, and a number of servants. She shared her childhood home with some very strange relatives. According to Marijane, "Louise had a grandmother and an aunt who threw money out of the window. The servants would catch it."

Though her background was wealthy and sophisticated, the abandonment and neglect she had suffered as a child left Louise very vulnerable as an adult. "She was resentful of almost every adult she ever came across," says Charlotte. "She would sit at Ursula's (editor-in-chief Ursula Nordstrom) desk hunched into herself, with a very belligerent look on her face, very vulnerable."

Charlotte vividly remembers working with Louise when she brought the first version of *Harriet the Spy* to Harper & Row. "When *Harriet the Spy* came in, it was more in the form of a short story," says Charlotte. "It wasn't a novel, it was a synopsis. But it was filled with such humor and such beautiful bits of dialogue, we knew there was a treasure in it." Louise came to see Ursula and Charlotte, and they started talking with her about how her manuscript could be made into a real book. "So many points that were raised in the original story were unfinished," says Charlotte. "We asked her, 'Why is the little girl so angry?'

" 'She's angry because her nursemaid went away and deserted her. She never wrote and she never came back,' said Louise.

"We said, 'But there is no nursemaid in the story you've shown us. Put her in.' We would question Louise intensely about many aspects like that. And in her answers we would often see entire chapters."

Writing did not come easily to Louise. "She kept notebooks. She agonized," remembers Marijane. "She rewrote. She loved suggestions. She was an editor's dream. She wanted help. She worked very hard on her writing."

Harriet the Spy was a breakthrough book, in Charlotte's opinion. "She showed that parents were normal human beings. Harriet's father came home from the office and called his friends ratfinks. That appalled the reviewers. Kids adored it. For the first time, they were reading a book that showed life as they saw it, not the way adults wanted them

> ## "Harriet the Spy has influenced more young people than Hemingway."
> —Charlotte Zolotow, Louise Fitzhugh's editor.

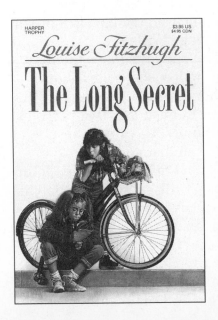

to." The reviewers also objected strongly to Harriet's spying activities, saying that endorsing a child's spying is a terrible thing to do. "We pointed out, as Louise did, that Harriet wanted to be a writer. That was why she was taking notes on everybody."

Many people have said that *Harriet the Spy* was ahead of its time and paved the way for such writers as Paul Zindel and Judy Blume. Marijane and Charlotte both thought that Louise never saw herself as a pathfinder. She just wrote her books the way she thought she should. "Underneath all her books there was a value system about life and people and politics that was very clear," says Charlotte.

Louise Fitzhugh died when she was just forty-six. Had she lived longer, she might have written many more important books. But those she did write will live long after her. "I've known dozens of kids who tried to dress like Harriet," says Charlotte. "After they read it, young people really do run around with their notebooks taking notes on things. It's the kids that will make that book last forever."

DO IT YOURSELF!

Carry around a notebook for a day, just as Harriet does. Take notes about things you hear, things you see, things you smell, taste, and feel. Take notes on conversations you have. At the end of the day, write a short story about what happened to you.

Jean Fritz

SELECTED TITLES

Born:
November 16, 1915, in Hankow, China

Home:
Dobbs Ferry, New York

Jean Fritz doesn't have to go searching for ideas, "My ideas find me," she says. "Ideas for books are a mixture of what comes in from the outside and what you are giving of yourself." Often, she decides to write a biography because she feels that "someone from the past is more or less saying, 'Write me.' "

When she researches the historical figures she writes about, she often looks for something quirky or unusual in that person's background. She thinks these details help her and her readers get to know the figure better. John Hancock's life shows these details. "He was always such a self-centered man, needing approval, always giving gifts. The larger the gift he gave, the greater his need for approval." Some children write her and say that they thought John Hancock was a big show-off. But Jean says, "When you read about his life and find out that he was an orphan who was adopted by a very rich uncle, you can see that he acted this way because he needed to. He did it becauses he was insecure."

When Jean is writing a historical novel, she takes voluminous notes. "I don't work from a very detailed outline," she says. "As I'm doing the research, the book more or less falls into shape. Then I write a very brief outline of where things are going to fit."

When she is writing a biography, she always goes to the place where the person lived. "This often turns up anecdotes and gives me a feeling for the person," she says.

THOSE WEE HOURS

Jean doesn't write with a computer, she writes by hand—very slowly. "I think a computer would intimidate me," she says. Jean usually works eight hours a day— a long, hard day for a writer. "When I get started on a book, I get quite obsessive about it. I can't get it out of my mind," she says. "I lie awake at night, going over lines, wondering what's coming next." She says, "Most of my creative work is done in those wee hours of the night when I want to be asleep. Things get solved when I am in a kind of going-to-sleep or trying-to-go-to-sleep mood that don't get solved sitting at a desk."

As she goes along, Jean rewrites a lot. "Every morning, I

read over everything I've done up to that point." She makes necessary changes then and there. Jean once commented, "By the law of averages, one would think there would be a certain percentage of sentences that would turn out right the first time. None of mine seem to, though."

When Jean ponders scenes from history, she gets very vivid pictures in her mind. Still, sometimes she finds the writing process frustrating. "I wish that I had all the actual dialogue to be able to put into the scene," she says. She knows a lot about the first time James Madison met his future wife, Dolly. "But I would love to have had the dialogue," says Jean. "I wonder how they managed the first time together, whether or not they laughed. I know he fell absolutely in love, but I wonder how the evening went. I have no idea. I can picture what they looked like, I know she was excited about her outfit, I even know that her best friend came over and helped her get dressed. But not knowing what they said bothers me. It makes me curious."

Jean's life was shaped by her childhood in China, where she lived until she was twelve. She went to an English school. Jean always felt very American and often spoke up for her country. "At recess, for instance, the English children would sometimes tease me by making fun of America. I never let that pass, even if it meant a fight. In history class, the teacher described our revolution as if it had just been a stupid American mistake. I didn't let that pass either."

She has often remarked that because she grew up so far away

Why don't you get a *horse*, SAM ADAMS?

by Jean Fritz
illustrated by Trina Schart Hyman

"I hope kids will read and get their parents to read to them. As soon as children can read, lots of parents abandon that practice. That's just too bad."

from America, she developed a homesickness that gave her a very deep feeling for its history. "No one is more patriotic than the one separated from his or her country," she wrote. "No one is as eager to find roots as the person who has been uprooted."

As a child, she was an avid reader. She recalls, "I don't know how my mother managed it, but she got all the good books for me. I had wonderful books as a child. I read all the time." She wrote a lot of "very poor poetry." She also kept a diary, which she started as a young teenager. She wishes she had started writing it earlier.

There are two activities that Jean always recommends to people interested in writing—especially children. "I always tell kids who like to write to keep a diary," she says. "It's a place to write things that happen, but also the kinds of feelings they're having. Anybody who wants to write has to be in touch with his or her own feelings. The time to get in touch with them is when you're in school, when you're young." Jean feels that too often students write what they think teachers or other adults would want, instead of asking themselves, "What's going on inside me?"

DO IT YOURSELF!

Here is a writing activity from Jean Fritz: "I think there is a great sense among children that grown-ups are a different breed. As a child, I remember wondering, How can I grow up to be that boring? That would be just awful. Later on, I realized that there are two kinds of adults—those who forget what it was to be a child and those who hang onto that memory. I think it would be interesting for children to write about how they think grown-ups look at something specific versus the way children look at the same thing."

Martyn Godfrey

SELECTED TITLES

The Vandarian Incident
1981

Alien War Games
1984

Here She Is, Ms. Teeny-Wonderful!
1985

Plan B Is Total Panic
1986

More than Weird
1987

Wild Night
1987

Can You Teach Me to Pick My Nose?
1990

Born:
April 17, 1949, in Birmingham, England

Home:
St. Albert, Alberta, Canada

Martyn Godfrey flunked third grade. "I couldn't write," he explains. "I couldn't spell, I couldn't put a sentence together. I didn't have a clue." But in seventh grade, things suddenly started clicking for him. Martyn can still recall doing a spelling lesson one day and realizing that it all made sense to him. "I guess that's just how my brain developed," he said. It was also in seventh grade that Martyn first began to enjoy creative writing.

LOTS OF CONTACT WITH KIDS

He went on to be a teacher, and he taught for eleven years until becoming a full-time writer in 1985. Constant contact with kids is still a part of his routine. "I have a class here in St. Albert, Alberta, which adopts me for the year," says Martyn. "I go in once a week. I talk to the kids. This helps me keep my mind open to things that they're doing."

Martyn also visits arcades. He goes to the fast-food part of his local mall and sits down to talk with kids. "I introduce myself and say, 'What are you up to? What's funny that's happened lately?' "

Quite often, the things kids tell him turn up in his books. "Whenever I use somebody's idea in one of my books, I also name one of the characters in the book after that person. It's my way of saying thanks," says Martyn.

"Often kids will ask me where I get ideas for specific scenes in my books," says Martyn. One scene he gets asked about a lot took place in his book *Can You Teach Me to Pick My Nose?* (Martyn points out that this is a book about skateboarding and that "nose picking" is a famous skateboarding trick.)

In that book, a boy gets his head stuck in his desk. Kids ask Martyn where he got the idea for that. "That actually happened to a fifth-grade student of mine," says Martyn. "We had indoor recess one day, because it was raining. This kid got down on his knees and decided to see if his head could fit in his desk. Once his head was in there, he panicked and tried to pull it out really quickly. He twisted his head, and his chin got caught. I heard him and helped him straighten out his head." Of course, when Martyn included the scene in his book, he made it a little more dramatic by having that event take place on the day that the superintendent was visiting that classroom.

Martyn writes all the time. "It's my life now," he says. "I can't separate Martyn Godfrey the writer from anything else I do anymore. Everything that happens to me becomes part of my writing." He works very hard on his writing. "I figured it out on the last two books I published," he says. "I logged the number of hours I spent writing and realized that by the time I finish revising, I've spend two hours on each page. I rewrite seven or eight times."

He writes his first two or three drafts on his computer, without even printing them out. Then he prints the book and reads it out loud to a wall in his house. "I want to know where the pitfalls are, where the story drags or is difficult to say or understand." After that, he takes the manuscript to his adopted classroom. He leaves. The teacher reads it out loud to the kids.

What kind of criticism does he get? "I find out if what I wrote is working. For example, I might work for ten pages to set up the funniest joke in the world. The kids don't get it or don't think it's funny. They smile or look away. Then, on the next page, there's the word *underwear*, and they laugh for five minutes." When that happens, he goes back to his "funniest joke in the world" and shortens the lead considerably.

After the manuscript has gone through these steps, he sends it to

APPLE PAPERBACKS

Scholastic
0-590-43416-7 / $2.75 US / $3.50 CAN

I SPENT MY SUMMER VACATION KIDNAPPED INTO SPACE

Oh, no!
They're about to be SLIMED!

Martyn N. Godfrey

"Make sure you grab your reader in the first couple sentences. Open your work with action, character, or dialogue."

his agent. "She's a very good critic at that point," he says. "She does the fine-tuning. By then I'm usually pretty confident about sending it away."

Martyn suggests that aspiring writers write as often as possible. He says, "I'm surprised at the number of adults who are aspiring writers but don't write every day." He further advises, "When describing things, forget about what they look like for a while. Don't tell me what it looks like, tell me what it smells or sounds like. Don't be afraid to throw more than one verb in a sentence. I think *She twisted and fell* is more exciting than *She twisted. She fell to the ground.* Put in slapstick."

When Martyn Godfrey visits a classroom, he always tells kids, "When you write, don't be afraid to lie about something that happened. We've all been in a classroom where somebody's fallen out of his chair for no reason at all. Tell the story, but lie a little. Say he falls out of his chair and scares the person next to him. She's so surprised that she throws her pencil in the air. Where does it land? In the substitute's coffee. *Exaggerate.*"

DO IT YOURSELF!

Here is a writing activity from Martyn Godfrey: "Imagine that you're in the wilderness and there's a bear charging at you. You've heard that if you play dead, the bear won't attack you. You drop down into the fetal position. Describe what happens next, using all of your senses except sight. What does the bear sound like? What do you feel? What does the bear's breath smell like? Does it smell rotten? Does it smell like blueberries? Without using any violence, describe the confrontation between the bear and you. Then share your story with a friend."

Virginia Hamilton

SELECTED TITLES

Zeely
1967

The House of Dies Drear
1970

*The Planet
of Junior Brown*
(Newbery Honor Book)
1972

*W. E. B. Dubois:
A Biography*
1972

M. C. Higgins, the Great
(Newbery Medal)
1974

Arilla Sun Down
1976

*Sweet Whispers,
Brother Rush*
1982

*The People Could Fly:
American Black Folktales*
1985

*In the Beginning:
Creation Stories from
Around the World*
(Newbery Honor Book)
1988

Cousins
1990

*The Dark Way: Stories
from the Spirit World*
1990

◆

Born:
March 12, 1936, in Yellow Springs, Ohio

Home:
Yellow Springs, Ohio, and New York, New York

Virginia Hamilton once had a vision of a boy running through the woods. That often happens when she begins writing a story. She explains, "A lot of times I will get a picture of something and then I follow the picture. I allow the emotion, then I use my intellect to limit or expand the picture. Not always, but sometimes, I sort of hear conversations, too."

In the instance Virginia cites, the running boy became M. C. Higgins, the protagonist of her Newbery-winning classic *M. C. Higgins, the Great*. "Often, characters come to me already fixed," she says. "The characters come up. I don't make them."

Though many of her novels are set in the area of Ohio where she has lived for most of her life, Virginia says that she does not write about events she has experienced or people she knows. "I try to distill experience, knowledge, fact, and memory into a kind of essence of what people are like," she says. "It's an essence of sights, sounds, smells, movement, experiences, mannerisms of people. They form a stew in my subconscious."

A LITTLE AFRAID

Most of the time, Virginia's writing flows smoothly. But *M. C. Higgins, the Great* was hard to write. "After *The Planet of Junior Brown* won all kinds of awards," she says, "I felt a lot of pressure. I was a little afraid to go on."

According to Virginia, the book that eventually won the Newbery Medal was vastly different from the book she started out to write. "What I wrote at first was empty." Virginia spent nine months rewriting the book, and along the way, she realized that she still had a lot to learn about its characters and subject matter. She recalls, "My characters weren't talking to each other. The focus wasn't there."

Although Virginia was very frustrated, she didn't walk away from the manuscript. She came to understand that she was trying to put too much in one book. She kept working on it, clarifying the characters and simplifying the story until she created the brilliant work that can be read today.

Over the years, Virginia has written many nonfiction books.

When she writes nonfiction, she has to do an enormous amount of research. "You have to know the material as well as you know yourself," she says. She finds all the material on her subject that she can get a hold of. She doesn't stop until she has covered all possible angles. She finds nonfiction harder to write than fiction. Why? "It's hard to keep all that stuff in your head long enough for it to come to life so you can write about it," she says.

Virginia Hamilton has some very good advice for aspiring writers: "Read as much as you can. Reading really does feed into writing. It seems to trip the imagination. You have to be very open, not afraid of words." She thinks those who like to write

should write every day, if possible. "When you're young, you think you have all the time in the world. You don't. Don't wait to be inspired. Just write."

"If you want children to like books, you should read out loud to them. It makes them think, 'I must be important because this person is taking all this time to read to me.' "

ODYSSEY
THE GATHERING
BOOK THREE IN THE JUSTICE CYCLE

BY NEWBERY MEDALIST
VIRGINIA HAMILTON

DO IT YOURSELF!

Here is a writing assignment that Virginia Hamilton used to give to her creative writing students: "Write a short mystery story that ends with this sentence: *There she lay, still as death, at the foot of the stairs.*" When you're done, read your story to some friends. Ask them to read their stories to you. Isn't it amazing how different each person's imagination is?

Monica Hughes

Born:
November 3, 1925, in Liverpool, England

Home:
Edmonton, Alberta, Canada

Monica Hughes believes that the events she has experienced sneak into her stories "through the back door of my subconscious—maybe through some external stimulus." She writes about things from ordinary life that she has a strong reaction to. For example, *Ring Rise, Ring Set* was set in a future ice age. "I wrote it at a time when there was a squabble about whether the world was heating up or cooling down," she says. *Devil on My Back* was written after she read a small article in a computer magazine that said that someday we might have microprocessors attached to our bodies. Her reaction to that idea? "Yuck."

When Monica comes across an idea that seems important, she writes it down. Then she files the ideas away. When she's between books, she goes through the file, "looking for something that sits up and says, 'Write me! Write me!' "

When she's thinking about writing a story but is not yet ready to write it, she spends a lot of time with a "pressure-cooker feeling." She says, "The whole thing is going around in my head and I write nothing. I burn the dinner. Slowly, a scenario or sometimes a character begins to emerge out of the mist and takes over and organizes things in my mind."

Often, she says, "I get a very, very clear flash, almost like a movie flash, of the first scene. It's visual and tactile. I can smell it. Everything comes across very, very clearly. Often a character will be there, too." She asks the char-

The Guardian of Isis by Monica Hughes

acter, "Who are you? Where were you before we met? Who were your parents?" Sometimes she sees the scene too. It might be an ocean or another planet. If she doesn't know much about the place she has imagined, she goes to the library and researches it.

"I was going to write a book about living under the sea," she says. "So I read about what it is like there. I found out about enormous forests of kelp—seventeen feet high. I thought, Someone could get lost in a forest of kelp." In that way, her research helps form her plot.

When Monica really knows the background of her story and has a sense of who the main characters are, she starts writing. Often, at first, she writes questions. "Sometimes the answers write themselves," she says. Then she writes an outline of what will happen in the chapters of the book. "When the characters start talking to each other or to me," she says, "I know it's time to begin the first draft."

She works quickly. "I have the personality profile that says closure is important," she says. By the time she begins to write a book, she usually wants it to end.

PAPER AND BLACK PENS

"I still use the same tools I started out with in 1971," she says, "loose-leaf binder paper and black pens. If I were stuck at home with a blue pen, I couldn't work."

Sometimes, she gets halfway through writing a book and finds she's stuck. "Then I go to my trusty word processor. I do it because I'm puzzled and can't read my own writing." Changing from pen and paper to a word processor sometimes gives her a new perspective. "It's like taking a sec-

> "When I write I have to be very free to receive images and ideas and yet still be in control. It's like driving a team of horses and giving them their lead, but not letting them run away in a totally wrong direction."

ond run up to the high jump," says Monica.

When she gets writer's block, she forces herself to stop and state what her story is about, who it is happening to and under what conditions. If she can't answer those questions, she stops and thinks some more. "Quite often writers are going on and writing the same thing over and over," she says. "Maybe then you're spinning your wheels. Maybe the story is over."

To help her imagine the worlds she's writing about, she often makes maps and charts. "I've always loved maps," says Monica. "When you leave a place that you know very well and head into the unknown, you're not able to visualize in the same way as usual." Maps and charts help her through this process.

Many of Monica's books are about ecological issues. "In many cases, I don't discover it until after I finish the book. Then I find out that the concerns of my regular life are seeping in." There is another relationship among many of her books as well—one she wasn't aware of until a teenager pointed it out to her: many of her heroines have red hair. "I was surprised to hear this," says Monica. "I went home and looked. At least four have red hair. It must be some sort of subconscious act of rebellion," she surmises. "Red hair makes a statement."

DO IT YOURSELF!

Here's a writing activity from Monica Hughes: "Write a story to go along with these sentences: *Two children are going through the forest when they find a trail. At the end of the trail is a hut. They go inside and find that it's perfectly furnished. On the shelf above the stove there is a . . .*"

E. L. Konigsburg

SELECTED TITLES

Jennifer, Hecate, Macbeth, William McKinley, and Me, Elizabeth
(Newbery Honor Book)
1967

From the Mixed-Up Files of Mrs. Basil E. Frankweiler
(Newbery Medal)
1967

About the B'nai Bagels
1969

A Proud Taste for Scarlet and Miniver
1973

The Second Mrs. Giaconda
1975

Father's Arcane Daughter
1977

Throwing Shadows
1979

Journey to an 800 Number
1982

Up from Jericho Tel
1986

Samuel Todd's Book of Great Colors
1989

Samuel Todd's Book of Great Inventions
1991

◆

Born:
February 10, 1930, in New York, New York

Home:
Jacksonville, Florida

All of her books are quite different from one another. But Elaine Lobl Konigsburg—or E. L. Konigsburg as she is known to her readers—has come to realize that they all have the same theme: the discovery of identity. Why is that her theme? "I don't know," she says. "I think I'm probably, even as a grandmother, still working out who I am."

EACH STORY IS UNIQUE

Though the themes are similar, each story is unique. "I did not realize until I finished *Father's Arcane Daughter*, which is as different as can be from *The Second Mrs. Giaconda*, the book preceding it, that both had the same theme: Who am I? What makes me the same as everyone else? What makes me different? I think those remain the central questions of young people."

To begin a day of writing, Elaine sits down in her book-filled study and "starts the movie" in her head. While she waits to be ready to write, she says, "I pick my thumbnails a lot." Writer's block strikes her occasionally. Then, she takes a long walk on the beach, or she draws or paints. She is an accomplished artist, and, with few exceptions, has illustrated all of her own books.

"I like to begin my story knowing my characters," Elaine says. "I know what they are going to do and how the story will end. I know an important episode in the middle. I don't always know how to get from A to B, but my characters often show me."

Elaine believes that her purpose in writing children's books is to take her readers somewhere. Her stories can be read on many levels. But she doesn't mind if readers miss her more complicated ideas. Elaine says, "When you write for children, you have an obligation to tell them a good story. There are some children who will only *get* the good story. There is only one reader in 10, 20, or 100 who gets the deeper part, the quest. Those who don't get it keep me grounded; those who do make me soar. Writers of children's books need both—roots and wings."

When offering advice to writers, Elaine always uses one word: *finish*. Here is the explanation: "I tell them that if they do finish, it means they have the essential ingredient other than talent—the discipline that it takes to apply the seat of their pants to the seat of their chair and get past that awkward transition and into the next paragraph, the next chapter. The difference between being a person of talent and being an author is the ability to finish."

Besides loving to write and read, Elaine enjoys giving talks. Recently, she gave a talk called "The Mask Beneath the Face." In it, she asked whether masks conceal or reveal. "I talked about a tribe in the Congo," she says. When a young boy of the Bapendes tribe is about to enter the tribe as an adult, he first goes through a

A DELL YEARLING BOOK   43180-8 • U.S. $3.25   CAN. $3.95

E.L. Konigsburg

From the Mixed-up Files of Mrs. Basil E. Frankweiler

The Newbery Award-winning classic

period of isolation, during which he constructs a mask representing the ghost of his childhood. "That just kills me," she says. Elaine wonders about her own mask: "What would it represent? How would it be colored? Would it be finished?" As a writer of children's books, she believes that her task is to help kids construct the masks of the ghosts of their childhoods. "The responsibility is awesome," she says.

> "I think I have changed as a result of each book I've written. When I have finished a book, I am no longer the person who started it, and part of the reason is because I wrote that book."

DO IT YOURSELF!

Here is an writing activity from E. L. Konigsburg: "Keep a journal. Use it to help you learn to write. Proper use of language shapes one's thinking. Sloppy language is not just a reflection of sloppy thinking; it produces sloppy thinking. The discipline of writing hones thinking skills."

Madeleine L'Engle

SELECTED TITLES

◆

Born:
November 29, 1918, in New York, New York

Home:
New York, New York

"When Johann Sebastian Bach was asked where he got his ideas for his music," says Madeleine L'Engle, "he explained that he just sat down to play and the music came out of him." In the same way, she has no idea where the stories she writes come from. They appear, and she writes them down.

"I JUST WRITE"

Madeleine doesn't think of herself as a children's writer at all. When people ask her why she writes for children, she answers, "I don't. I just write. If the book is particularly complicated, then, of course, children are going to enjoy it more than adults."

Having gone to an English boarding school, with little priva-cy and many distractions, Madeleine can now write anywhere. When she travels, she carries a portable computer with her and even writes on airplanes and in hotel rooms. She writes in the morning, even though some days she doesn't really want to. "If you just write when you feel like it, you're not going to have much," she says. "The inspiration comes while you're writing." She says that sometimes the hardest part of her day is just sitting down and getting started.

When she finishes the draft of a book, Madeleine starts rewriting it immediately. "I love to rewrite, particularly if I know what's happening," she says. "I realize what I need to do that I haven't done, and I love to get at it and do it. It's exciting." Through revision, she says, her story deepens. She discovers more about her characters.

The book she's writing now is a novel for adults. It started out to be about King David's eight wives. She decided to add a twentieth-century point of view. After three rewrites (she's on her fourth), her twentieth-century cast has taken over, and her original idea is now a play that one of the women characters is writing. She says that she now knows that it is a novel about creativity and forgiveness. "With this book I felt as though I'd been given a great chunk of granite and a little, tiny chisel and a little, tiny hammer to tap-tap away to find out what's inside."

Madeleine reads all the time. Sometimes she reads murder mysteries. Sometimes she reads books about particle physics. She first became interested in physics when she began to read the writing of Albert Einstein, just before she wrote *A Wrinkle in Time*. She says, "I was looking for a theology I could believe in, and I read one of Einstein's books in which he said: 'Anyone who's not lost in rapturous joy at the power of the mind behind the universe is as good as a burnt-out candle.' I thought, I've found my theologian."

Though Madeleine has been a successful writer for more than thirty years, she once lived through a period of ten years when she didn't sell anything. *A Wrinkle in Time*, her most popular book of all, was rejected by countless publishers, who couldn't decide if the book was for children or adults. And they were afraid to take a chance with it.

Madeleine sometimes reflects on her years of rejection. "I cried," she remembers. "I'd walk the dogs down the dirt road at night after I put the kids to bed, and I would cry. It was hard. It was very hard. I lost faith in myself and I lost a lot of my *joie de vivre*. My essence was not being accepted. There was a whole part of my being that was not being accepted, and it was hurt, and that was hard.

"I don't know how much longer I could have gone on if *Wrinkle* hadn't been published," she continues. "I don't know if I could have kept faith in myself." Luckily, those years are now far behind her.

The Newbery Award—winning Classic
A WRINKLE IN TIME
Madeleine L'Engle

When asked what advice she gives to kids who like to write, Madeleine L'Engle says: "One: Keep an honest, unpublishable journal that you don't show to anybody, because what you write down you tend not to forget. By writing in a journal, you're keeping track of your life. And you're having a say in your own life story. Two: Read. Three: Write. Don't be afraid. Just go out and do it."

> "I don't think everybody has to write. We need readers. And I think the reader grossly underestimates his or her importance in bringing a book to life. Reading is a creative activity. You have to visualize the characters, you have to hear what their voices sound like."

DO IT YOURSELF!

Here is a writing activity from Madeleine L'Engle: "When I give a writer's workshop, I say, 'Start writing. Don't think. Just write. And you may not write for more than an hour.'" Try Madeleine's assignment. You'll probably be pleasantly surprised by the results.

Jean Little

Born:
January 2, 1932, in Taiwan

Home:
Guelph, Ontario, Canada

A young girl once interrogated Jean Little intensely. She asked the same question over and over: How do you know how to do it?

"That was one question I couldn't answer," admits Jean. "I thought it was quite an easy question to answer until I tried. I *know* how I do it, but I don't know *how* I know how I do it. That's what separates the creative people from everybody else. Mozart didn't know how he knew how to write music." Jean kept trying to answer the child, but every time she got to the end of her response, the girl would repeat, "But how do you know how to do it?" Jean was never able to answer the question to the girl's satisfaction.

Without knowing how she knows how she does it, Jean Little has been writing since she was ten years old. As a child, she was something of an outsider. Her closest friends were her brothers and her sister. Jean's isolation may have stemmed in part from the fact that she was different: she had crossed eyes and was extremely short-sighted. Now she is legally blind.

Getting around has always been a problem for Jean. But by holding books very close to her face, she could read. She held the books so close to her face that her nose often turned black from rubbing in the ink. "My friends were the people in books," she explains. She read her favorites over and over, especially *A Secret Garden* by Frances Hodgson Burnett, a book she read so often that her copy finally fell to pieces. "And I always reread *The Little Princess*, also by Frances Hodgson Burnett, which has the best ending of any book I've ever read." She still reads a lot, but she relies on talking books.

A CHILD OF MISSIONARIES

When Jean began to write professionally, she remembered how lonely she had been in her childhood. Those memories inspired one of her most popular books, *From Anna*. Here is how she arrived at the idea for the book: "When I was seven I was in a sight-saving class in Toronto. I wove a basket for my parents. In high school, I wrote a short story about a little girl who did that.

But as I kept working on the story, I decided that the little girl couldn't be me. My family history was too complicated." (Jean was the child of missionaries and spent the first part of her childhood in Asia.) So Jean gave her character a different family background and changed her in other ways. But in one important way, she and Anna are similar. "Her feelings about her vision are the same as mine," says Jean.

Though many physically challenged children respond to Jean's books, those aren't the ones she's really writing for. "When I write about physically challenged children," she says, "I write more for those children who are not, so that they can see that all children are really alike." But she tries never to make her point too strongly. "Books with one big fat message I don't like," she says firmly.

When Jean first started writing, she was able to see well enough to read what she wrote or typed. But

by the time she wrote *Mama's Going to Buy You a Mockingbird*, her eyes were no longer strong enough for that. She created that book by talking into a tape recorder and having somebody else type it up. "It took me six and a half years to write that book," she remembers. "It was terrible, really difficult, to make structural changes. The editors wanted me to take a character out, and I had to go through all thirty-five tapes to do it."

When computers, and in particular talking computers, were invented, "it was just like a miracle," says Jean. Now she writes by typing in her text, and from time to time has the computer read the text back to her.

When writing, Jean likes to get inside the minds of her characters. "I have to remind myself to put the visual descriptions in, because I like them when I read. But when I'm actually writing, I'm not picturing the story much. I'm always inside the main character's head."

When she gets stuck, she tries to keep writing, "even if it's garbage." Usually she can get past a block in that way.

To those who like to write, Jean Little advises: "Some people can, and some people can't. The way you learn is by reading a lot. I don't know a single writer who doesn't read and write a lot. You have to practice to get better at it."

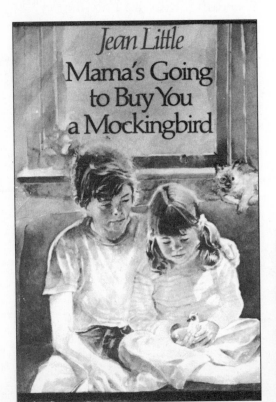

DO IT YOURSELF!

Jean Little suggests this writing activity: "Pretend you're telling a story to a friend. As you tell the story, write down what you're saying. Or, pretend you're watching the story that's in your imagination on television. What do you see? Write it down."

Lois Lowry

SELECTED TITLES

◆

Born:
March 20, 1937, in Honolulu, Hawaii

Home:
Boston, Massachusetts

L ois Lowry has said that composing a story is like piecing patches of a quilt together, combining scenes and dialogue to make a colorful, meaningful whole. Though most of her books have come from her imagination, two of them, *Autumn Street* and *A Summer to Die*, came directly from her own experiences. And her Newbery-winning *Number the Stars* came from the childhood experiences of a good friend, which she combined with historical facts.

A LIVELY IMAGINATION

"Often kids send me ideas, particularly for the *Anastasia* series," she says. "Though I may use a general idea sent by a child, I always veer off into my imagination to enhance and embellish the plot."

Lois writes in a small studio apartment near her Beacon Hill, Boston, home. Some of the walls of her cozy office are lined with bookcases; others are covered with photographs (she has also worked as a photographer). Hanging over her desk is an oil painting of herself reading in her garden in New Hampshire (where she spends weekends in an old farmhouse) painted by an artist friend. She always listens to classical music while she works.

She writes on a word processor, revising as she goes along. "It all just comes out of my head into the computer," says Lois. "There is a lot of rewriting, but because it takes place throughout the process—each day I go back and rewrite the previous day's work—it is difficult to tell how many

rewrites I do." When she finishes her first draft, she prints it out and then goes back and rewrites it again, from beginning to end.

Lois considers herself a very visual writer. "No surprise that I was once a photographer," she says. She always has very clear pictures in her mind when she writes. But she doesn't expect readers' imaginations to create the same pictures that she has seen. "One of the gratifying things about books is that they allow each reader to create his or her own world," she says.

There is always *something* to write about, Lois believes, so writer's block has never bothered her much. On days when her book-writing doesn't get off to a fast start, she can always answer fan mail instead. "I get hundreds of letters from kids," she says. "Just the act of sitting and typing, even if it is only letter answering, nudges me into creativity."

Lois describes herself as having been a quiet, introspective, shy child. She says she was "a book-worm who was always reading." She also wrote from the time she was very young. "But in my day, at least in my town, my school, there was very little, if any, encouragement of creativity." So she wrote for her own enjoyment—something she still does. As a child, she wrote poems and stories—"none of them particularly wonderful"—that brought her a great deal of satisfaction. She rarely showed what she wrote to anyone else.

Once, when she was speaking to a big group of teachers and librarians, Lois was asked what her purpose was in writing for adolescents. "I answered that it was to make the reader feel less

"When I write, I draw a great deal from my own past. There is a satisfying sense of continuity, for me, in the realization that my own experiences, fictionalized, touch young readers in subtle and very personal ways."

Lois Lowry
ALL ABOUT SAM
With illustrations by Diane deGroat

alone," she says, adding, "I remember feeling irritated at the person for asking what seemed an unanswerable question and at myself, for having answered it hastily and, I thought, inadequately." But on reflection, Lois Lowry decided that her answer was not so bad after all. "Adolescence is often a painfully lonely time," she believes. "It is a time when communication is difficult. A book can be a vehicle for communication; and a book can alleviate the sense of isolation that sometimes makes growing up lonely. Walking through a scary place is easier if you know that someone else has walked there once and survived."

DO IT YOURSELF!

Here is a writing activity from Lois Lowry: "I always tell would-be writers to search their own memories for a time when they experienced a strong emotion: fear, anger, joy, sorrow, guilt. How, as a result of the experience that created that emotion, did they change? There is where a story lies."

David Macaulay

SELECTED TITLES

◆

Born:
December 2, 1946, in Burton-on-Trent, England

Home:
Providence, Rhode Island

David Macaulay fondly remembers walking to school in his childhood home of Bolton, England. "One of the great things was the twenty-minute walk through the woods to school each day. I was very familiar with the area, since it was my playground when I was not in school. It allowed me to let my mind wander."

A CHILDHOOD FILLED WITH PLAY

His English childhood was idyllic and filled with play. It was also filled with inventions. He loved to build elevators out of cigar boxes, string, and tape. He used yarn to make complicated systems of moving cable cars. "I would take my little soldiers into the sitting room, put them in the flowerpots, and with threads and spools construct cable cars from the top of the curtain rods down to the corner of the room. I created a crazy spiderweb of threads on which I occasionally tied up soldiers, taking them for terrifying rides." In 1957 David and his family moved to America. "Moving to the States was an incredible shock," he says. "I wore long pants for the first time in my life."

He felt much younger than the kids around him. "Life was faster and my contemporaries seemed more mature," he says. "Looking back, I wonder how many of them had the benefit of an extended childhood, which I had had." He says that his childhood came to an end between the sixth and seventh grades, "but my imagination never stopped protecting me, coming back into play when I needed it."

David Macaulay went to college at the prestigious Rhode Island School of Design, where he studied architecture. "Architecture teaches you how to tackle any problem of any scale," he says. "It fueled and educated my desire to understand how things work." He realizes that what he learned in architecture—"how to break down an immense problem into its smallest parts and put it back together logically with knowledge, expertise, and imagination"— also applied to the process of making books.

He always liked to draw. In fact, he can still remember his first successful drawing of a fire engine. "I think I was eight at the time," he says. It was the first drawing he ever did that elicited a strong reaction. "It was a very positive reaction and very reassuring. It was also addicting. I have never stopped wanting to know how other people are reacting to my work; in fact, I sometimes wonder if I ever draw for myself."

Before beginning any book, David spends months doing research. For *Cathedral*, he spent time in France photographing Gothic cathedrals. *Pyramid* took him to Egypt, where he stood on top of the Great Pyramid. "It was something that I wanted to do in order to draw it more convincingly. I had to have a sense of what it felt like as well as what it looked like," David recalls. Although it is illegal to climb the Great Pyramid, David persuaded the authorities to make an exception. And at seven o'clock in the morning, he stood on top of it. "The single most impressive image was the length of the shadow it cast. The sun was just coming up and the shadow went on forever across the desert."

In his pictures, David always tries to make the reader more of a participant than a spectator. "I want him up on the roof of the building, and I want him to feel slightly sick because it's a long way up." David says that if a reader can share the experience of being involved in a process, he will remember it. "If I have any expertise at all, it is in that kind of communication," he believes.

Making sure his pictures are accurate requires a tremendous, sometimes tiresome, amount of fact-checking. "Every time I finish a picture I have to go back and check it with the previous ten pictures to make sure there are no

"I can draw buildings with my eyes closed, but the better I get at drawing buildings, the worse my people and animals look. I drew an ox in *City* that looks like a walking refrigerator."

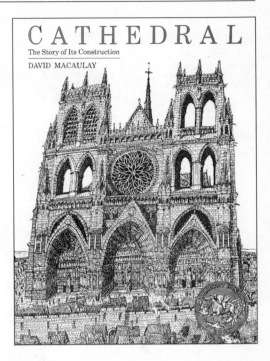

inconsistencies," explains David. "You become the continuity person as well as the creator and the illustrator." This aspect of the work exhausts him. "It goes on for the entire process of making the book, which could be as long as six months."

By then, he is no longer as excited as he was at the beginning. When a project is completed, he is very relieved. "The fun lies in developing the idea and creating a fluid framework for both words and pictures."

DO IT YOURSELF!

One of David Macaulay's most interesting books is called *Unbuilding*. It is about disassembling the Empire State Building (which, so far, has only happened in David's imagination). To find out how the building would be taken down, David first had to learn how it was built. Find out how an object was put together—it could be something as complicated as a car or as simple as a table. Write the instructions for putting the object together. Try to write with as much clarity as possible. Then, reverse the instructions and explain how to take the object apart.

Patricia MacLachlan

SELECTED TITLES

Arthur, for the Very First Time
1980

Tomorrow's Wizard
1982

Cassie Binegar
1982

Unclaimed Treasures
1984

Sarah, Plain and Tall
(Newbery Medal)
1985

The Facts and Fictions of Minna Pratt
1988

Journey
1991

◆

Born:
March 3, 1938, in Cheyenne, Wyoming

Home:
In the Berkshire Mountains of western Massachusetts

Patricia MacLachlan thinks that writers are really spies. "A writer hears something or sees something and uses it," she says. She agrees with the poet and essayist Robert Penn Warren, who once said that a writer writes to answer a question. She adds, "I can't write anything that doesn't have some connection to what I care about."

Though her stories are often based in fact, they are always colored by her imagination. "My parents taught me that while things in books are not always factual, they do hold truth and are important," says Patricia. She looks for those elements when she reads and writes books.

Patricia was an only child who was always curious. She was also an avid reader. She says, "When I was young, my mother would lead me home from the library as I read, her hand on my neck, guiding me across streets and up and down curbs. By the time I got home, my books were all finished and it was time to return to the library for more." She says she still reads that way. She also remembers, "My father would invite me into books, playing the characters, acting out scenes with such dedication and zest that books became every bit as real, and as important, as life each day."

Patricia had a strong fantasy life, with many make-believe brothers and sisters. "That's how I learned to play out themes, to develop characters, to hear other voices," she explains. Today, she still reads everything she writes out loud. "I need to have the voices of the characters whisper in my ear."

INTERESTING QUESTIONS

Patricia often visits schools, and she is interested in the questions students ask her. "They often ask me if my stories are true," she says. "Then we get into a discussion about what truth is." She has also noticed that more kids than ever are writing, which she's happy about. But she is discouraged that many kids are not patient writers. "Television has created a whole generation of people who live in fleeting moments," she says. "Kids don't have the patience they need to sit and work through an entire book."

A kid once asked her, "Why is my idea better in my head than on paper?" Patricia thought that was a very sophisticated question. "I answered that I have the same problem sometimes."

She doesn't believe in writer's block, though. "When you can't write, there's a reason for it," she says. "Maybe you have to stop and think about it." She calls those spells back-burner time, because they happen when something needs to sit for a little bit.

Patricia MacLachlan writes with an electric typewriter. "I have a computer, but it makes me cry," she says. "I haven't learned to use it." She types each page over and over again, until it pleases her, and then she goes on to the next one.

"My writing process is organic," she says. "It grows from the beginning up—from the soil up into the air. I may know at the beginning how I want it to end. But the whole middle part of getting there I work through as I go." Though she knows that most

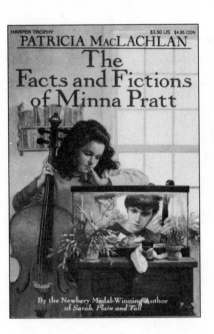

"When I drive along in my car, I have conversations with my characters. People think I'm singing along with the radio."

teachers advise their students to write from an outline, she never uses one. "There is no right way to write," she says. She believes that each writer must learn to bring out her voice in her own way.

Patricia is a very visual writer. "I tend to write as if I were looking through a movie camera," she explains. "My scenes open and close, my chapters rise and fall, just like a movie script." She thinks this ability may actually limit her in some ways. "I cannot write about a place I've never been and don't know," she says. "I am so grounded, I have to know what the land looks like, the color of the sky, in each of my stories."

Before she starts writing a new book, Patricia MacLachlan reads really good books by writers such as Natalie Babbitt, William Steig, and E. B. White. "They put me on the track of how language ought to be," she says. Books have always been the strongest force in Patricia's life. There are books in every room of her house. "My greatest fear is being stuck somewhere without a book," she says.

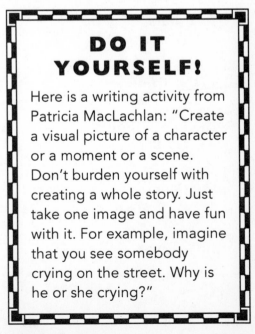

DO IT YOURSELF!

Here is a writing activity from Patricia MacLachlan: "Create a visual picture of a character or a moment or a scene. Don't burden yourself with creating a whole story. Just take one image and have fun with it. For example, imagine that you see somebody crying on the street. Why is he or she crying?"

Margaret Mahy

SELECTED TITLES

Born:
March 21, 1936, in Whakatane,
New Zealand

Home:
Lyttleton, New Zealand

When Margaret Mahy was a child, she wanted animals to like her. She drew on that memory to write *The Boy Who Was Followed Home*, but she exaggerated it, of course. She could have written about a boy who was followed home by guinea pigs. But she thought it would be funnier if he were followed home by a startling number of hippopotamuses. Her stories often have a basis in reality. But, she admits, "I do, in a way, change the events."

DETERMINED TO BE A WRITER

As a child, Margaret was something like the character Tabitha in *The Haunting*: fair-haired, very talkative, and determined to be a writer. She started writing when she was about seven. Her mother saved the first story she ever wrote. "It was about a boy called Harry who was very lazy," Margaret remembers. "One day, he followed a golden pheasant to the house of a witch. The witch made him work for her. If he didn't, she'd beat him with a broomstick. When he got over being lazy, she asked him to go home. At the end, he woke up. It was a dream. It's got a good structure," she says, content that her first work showed a glimmer of promise.

When Margaret was at school, she had two other friends who liked to write. "Now writing is part of the school program," she says. "But then we had to write after school because we wanted to do it ourselves." Her friends stopped writing in high school, but Margaret kept on. "It's quite important to persist, in spite of disappointments," she believes.

Margaret works in her bedroom, at a long bench that holds a word processor, a fax machine, a photocopier, and a laser printer. "My cats like to sleep on the fax machine and the laser printer," she says. "The machines are a little bit warm. The cats curl up on them." The room is filled with things that interest her, such as a favorite painting and stones from different places. "It's a pretty happy clutter, though sometimes it gets a bit hectic," she admits.

Now she does most of her writing on a word processor. But she used to write on lined paper, skipping every other line. When she went back to revise, she would write in different colors, "so the crowded words in the middle of the lines would be easier to read." She did it to entertain herself too. "When the page became so untidy that I couldn't read the story, I'd type it for the first time," says Margaret. "The minute I typed it out, I'd find there was a lot wrong with it. Then with clear print on the page, I'd start correcting it again."

One of the most challenging books Margaret has written is *The Tricksters*. "There were twelve characters that had to be acknowledged and developed," she says. "There were times when I wondered, What's gone wrong with this book? I slowly realized that the problem was that I had to give so many characters something to say, some sort of force in the story, and some sort of position to hold." Recognizing that the task was a difficult one gave her the encouragement to tackle it again.

By the time Margaret starts writing a story, she usually knows how it will begin and end, more or less—"though there are parts in the middle I'm not too sure about." Sometimes she sees pictures in her mind when she writes, but more often she hears a voice telling her the story. "I think quite a lot about the stories I write," she says.

She likes to travel and to meet other writers and her readers. She also likes to talk about storywriting with children. "In Ohio, I met a boy who asked why it was that stories always ended well for the good people and badly for the bad people," says Margaret. "I thought that was an interesting question. I answered that most of the time,

"Most people's lives are made up of good parts and bad parts. Most writers choose to end the story at a positive time for the hero or heroine, but that's not the real end of the story."

ALIENS IN THE FAMILY
MARGARET MAHY

stories end up well for the good people because although stories are set up to entertain us, they are also expected to strengthen us." She adds, "Many folktales deal with the triumph of a good, kind, simple person rather than a rich, powerful, clever person. Folktales are one of the ways people make sense of their own lives."

DO IT YOURSELF!

Here is a writing activity from Margaret Mahy: "Take some real thing that's happened to you and turn it into a fantastic story. For example, once I drove off the road. People driving by stopped to see if they could help me. The first four said they wouldn't be able to help me get my car out of the ditch. But the next person that came along said, 'It's only a little car, let's lift it up.' So we stood around and lifted the car out of the ditch. You could retell this story in a very realistic fashion, or you could change it a little. Maybe it could become a story about a king who went off the road and got stuck in a ditch. Animals could come along to help him: a big blue buffalo, a snake on a skateboard—even a snake on a *snake*board."

Walter Dean Myers

SELECTED TITLES

◆

Born:
August 12, 1937, in Martinsburg,
West Virginia

Home:
Jersey City, New Jersey

In Walter Dean Myers's workroom hangs a favorite object
that changes with each project
he works on. It is a collage his
artist wife made for him, full of
material related to whatever story
he happens to be writing. When
he begins a new project, he and
his wife collect objects and pictures, and she puts them together.
Besides providing a decoration for
his office, the collage serves
another important purpose. "It
helps me visualize my story," he
says. "My major weakness as a
writer is in visualization. Left to
my own devices, I could have a
character think for eight pages."

A PLUMBER OF SORTS

The collage is a hint at how devot-
ed Myers is to his craft, and how
hard he works. He doesn't take

himself very seriously, though. "I
think of myself as more of a
plumber," he says. "That's not a
bad thing. You have to put the
work into it. This idea that you
have to be talented I'm not sure
about. I haven't decided if I have
any talent or not. But I work hard.
Not working hard enough is how
most people fail."

Myers has been interested in
writing since he was a teenager. "I

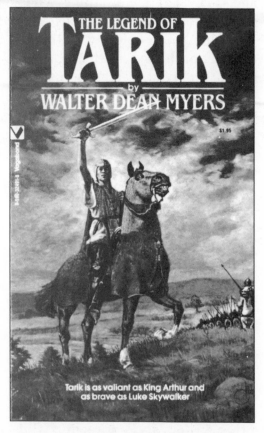

Tarik is as valiant as King Arthur and
as brave as Luke Skywalker

wrote about all the 'capital' stuff,"
he says. "Life. Death." He laughs
about a story he wrote back then.
The story began like this: *The
lonely stranger got off the bus.* He
says, "I had no idea where I was
going to go. I just thought, This is
going to be so deep and so heavy,

it's going to knock everybody out. This was what I thought writing was."

Now, he knows better. "Planning to put a book together is hard work." He feels that whenever he doesn't do the necessary thinking, the book suffers. "When I get to the part that's not thought through, I stumble my way through it. The editor always knows." So now, before he begins each book, he spends a while thinking about it. He has found that if he does a good job of thinking a book through before he starts it, he will spend less time rewriting later.

Walter never writes to try to help kids solve their problems. "When I do that, I blow it." He gets his ideas from newspapers and from things that bother him. "If something bothers me or gives me a problem somehow, I'll eventually turn that into a story. I'll do a book looking for the answer."

For example, the seeds for *Fallen Angels*, Walter's award-winning book about the Vietnam War, were sown when his brother was killed in 1968. "I thought and thought about what happened to him." Eventually, when Walter's editor, Jean Feiwel, asked him to write a book about going into the army, he was finally ready to write about what happened to his brother in Vietnam.

Walter Dean Myers likes to write. "I don't mind that it's difficult," he says. "People say they hate writing. I think it's nonsense. Sure, it's hard. I've had hard jobs

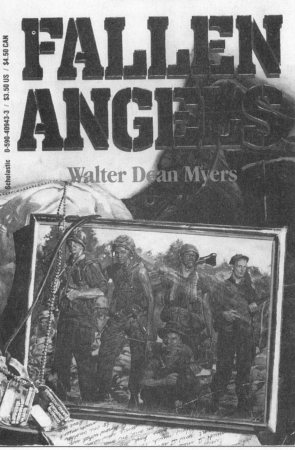

"It is a tale that is as thought-provoking as it is entertaining...."
—*The New York Times*

FALLEN ANGELS

0-590-40943-3 / $3.50 US / $4.50 CAN   Scholastic

Walter Dean Myers

in my life. I remember when I spent days tearing down the interior of a building in New York City. I used a sledgehammer. When I'd go to sleep at night, my whole body would cramp up. *That* was hard. *This* is easy."

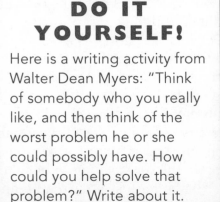

DO IT YOURSELF!

Here is a writing activity from Walter Dean Myers: "Think of somebody who you really like, and then think of the worst problem he or she could possibly have. How could you help solve that problem?" Write about it.

"As a kid, I was taught that people like Shakespeare and Milton, all these wonderful, brilliant dudes, stood on the moor and the wind went through them and came out the other side as poetry. I thought if I had to *think* about it, if it didn't come naturally, I wasn't talented."

Scott O'Dell

SELECTED TITLES

Island of the Blue Dolphins
(Newbery Medal)
1961

The King's Fifth
(Newbery Honor Book)
1967

The Black Pearl
(Newbery Honor Book)
1968

Sing Down the Moon
(Newbery Honor Book)
1971

Child of Fire
1974

The Hawk That Dare Not Hunt by Day
1975

Zia
1976

Streams to the River, River to the Sea: A Novel of Sacajawea
1986

The Serpent Never Sleeps: A Novel of Jamestown and Pocahontas
1987

Black Star, Bright Dawn
1988

My Name Is Not Angelica
1989

◆

Born:
May 23, 1898, in Los Angeles, California

Died:
October 15, 1989

Scott O'Dell, who died in 1989, wrote about places he knew. "I always visit a place I am going to write about," he said. "That gives me the true feeling of the locale, the weather, the land, the sky, and the people who once lived there."

BORN IN A FRONTIER TOWN

Scott O'Dell was born on Terminal Island, which is part of Los Angeles. "Los Angeles was a frontier town when I was born there around the turn of the century," he wrote. "It had more horses than automobiles, more jackrabbits than people. The very first sound I remember was a wildcat scratching on the roof as I lay in bed."

His father was a railroad man, so Scott moved around a lot as a child. Many of the places he lived showed up his is books as settings in his stories. For a time, he lived on Rattlesnake Island, across the bay from San Pedro, California, in a house perched on stilts over the water. "The waves came up and washed under us every day," he wrote. "And sailing ships went by. That is why, I suppose, the feel of the frontier and the sound of the sea are in my books."

Many of Scott's books were set in the past, but the issues that he dealt with are timeless. "The problems of isolation, moral decisions, greed, and need for love and affection are problems of today as well. I am didactic—I do want to teach through books," he confessed.

Scott O'Dell thought that writing historical fiction for children was very important work. "Children have a strong feeling that they sprang full-grown from the forehead of Jove. Anything of the past is old hat. But no educated person can live a complete life without a knowledge of where we came from. History has a direct bearing on children's lives," he said.

Perhaps Scott's most well-known book is the Newbery-winning *Island of the Blue Dolphins*. That story takes place on some islands that are much like those he lived on as a kid. Scott put many of his happy childhood memories in that book: the look of the islands; the colors and sounds of the sea; and the wild creatures that lived there.

The book was also inspired in

part by a disturbing memory from his childhood. He and his friends used to climb the mountains to the east of Los Angeles, capture owls, and kill them. As a boy, he did not understand the cruelty of the act.

But as a man, Scott was outraged at himself and at others who harm animals. He wrote the book in anger: "anger at the hunters who invade the mountains where I live and who slaughter everything that creeps or walks or flies. This anger was also directed at myself, at the young man of many years ago, who thoughtlessly committed the same crimes against nature."

Scott thought that writing for children was more rewarding than writing for adults. "Children have the ability that most adults have lost, the knack to be someone else, of living through

stories and lives of other people." Having written both for children and adults, he noticed that "six months after the publication of an adult novel, there's a big silence. Or so it is with me. But with a book for children, it's just the opposite. If children like your book they respond for a long time, with thousands of letters. It is this response, this concern and act of friendship, that for me makes the task of writing worth doing." During his lifetime, Scott O'Dell usually received more than 2,000 letters a year from his young readers.

When Scott wasn't writing, he liked to read and to work in the sun. He enjoyed gardening, planting trees, and fishing. He said, "I like watching the weather, the seabirds, the whales moving north and south with the seasons, the dolphins and all the life of the changing waters."

> "The stories that have been written by great writers possess lives of their own. They live through the years and through the centuries. They are as substantial as mountains, more lasting than habitations."

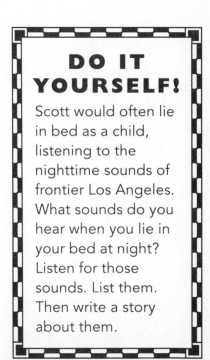

DO IT YOURSELF!

Scott would often lie in bed as a child, listening to the nighttime sounds of frontier Los Angeles. What sounds do you hear when you lie in your bed at night? Listen for those sounds. List them. Then write a story about them.

Katherine Paterson

SELECTED TITLES

◆

Born:
October 31, 1932, in Qing Jiang, Jiangsu, China

Home:
Barre, Vermont

"The old idea was that you have to live an exciting life to write good books," says Katherine Paterson. "I believe that you have to have a very rich imaginative life. You don't have to fight dragons to write books. You just have to live deeply the life you've been given."

Katherine's "deeply lived" life has taken her all over the world. Her early childhood was spent in China, where her father was a missionary. During World War II, she was evacuated with her family. They came to live in North Carolina, where Katherine's odd clothes and unusual British accent made her an outcast. As a result, she became an avid reader with a very vivid fantasy life.

Many of Katherine's books deal with very difficult subjects. Kids often ask her how she feels when she's writing about things that are sad or frightening. Katherine answers, "It rips me up. If something terrible happens to my characters, I'm in agony."

A sixth-grader once asked her: "If it's so painful to you, why do you do it?" Katherine answered, "I'm not quite sure why, except that I think the books I've loved the most are the books that make me experience the entire spectrum of life. They make me laugh and cry and worry. They frighten me. Everything that a person would normally experience in a lifetime is encapsulated between the covers of such a book. That's the type of book you love.

"When we moved from Maryland to Virginia, our youngest child was throwing up, she was so upset. She told me, 'I never had any practice moving.' That's what books do for you. They give you practice doing difficult things in life. In a way, they prepare you for things that you are going to have to face or someone you know and care about is going through. They sort of help you know how it feels—though not exactly. It is the remove that gives you a deep pleasure rather than a total pain."

THE WONDER OF BOOKS

Not all of the sad or painful parts of her books reach all kids. "One of the wonders of books is that the reader gets what she's ready to get when she's reading it." But often children will tell Katherine, "I didn't get it the first time, but when I read it *again* . . ." That makes Katherine beam. "What a compliment!"

Katherine writes first on a typewriter and then revises on a computer. Usually, after she finishes her first draft, she lets the book sit for at least three weeks. "I'd probably think it was awful if I went right back to it. My first draft is always a mess. I'd become so discouraged I'd want to pitch it rather than rewrite." If she lets it sit, she can see what she was really trying to do. "The time to start rewriting is when you can look at it and say, 'Not bad.' "

She thinks that everyone should write. "It's a way of getting

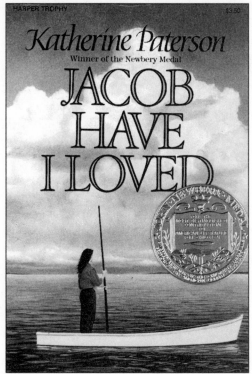

person who's whining and wailing to get it on paper."

Though Katherine Paterson enjoys visiting kids in schools, she doesn't like it when teachers say to her, "We want the children to see that authors are real, live people." Katherine says, "I think that's feeding into the celebrity sickness we have in this country. It implies that if you are a celebrity, everybody else is a nobody. Children should learn that they are somebody, no matter what. Each of us has to prize who we are and love that person."

> **"When people ask what qualifies me to be a writer for children, I say I was once a weird little kid. I'm sure there are plenty of fine writers who have overcome the disadvantages of a normal childhood. It's just that we weird little kids do seem to have a head start."**

your feelings out and looking at them," she says. She doesn't believe everyone should be published, though: "You have to have some shape," she says. "It's boring to read somebody else's whines and wails. But it's helpful to the

DO IT YOURSELF!

Here is a writing activity from Katherine Paterson: "Somebody once sent me Agnes Stokes's diary. [Agnes Stokes is the scrawny little girl who attaches herself to Gilly in Katherine's book *The Great Gilly Hopkins*.] The diary tells the story from her point of view. I loved it. The kid did a wonderful job. It was Agnes looking at Gilly, rather than Gilly looking at Agnes. Try to write a story from an unlikable character's point of view."

Gary Paulsen

SELECTED TITLES

Winterkill
1977

Tiltawhirl John
1977

Hope and a Hatchet
1978

The Green Recruit
1980

The Spitball Gang
1980

Tracker
1984

Dogsong
(Newbery Honor Book)
1985

Murphy
1987

The Crossing
1987

Hatchet
(Newbery Honor Book)
1988

The Winter Room
(Newbery Honor Book)
1990

The River
1991

◆

Born:
May 17, 1939, in Minneapolis, Minnesota

Home:
Becida, Minnesota

G ary Paulsen can't just make stuff up. To write a book, he says, "I kind of live it." *Hatchet*, his novel about a boy's survival experience after a plane crash, is a good example. "I have lived through two forced landings in bush planes," he says. "I have done all the survival things in the book the way the boy did." Except one. "I had never built a fire using only a hatchet, so I did it. It took me quite a while, but I did it." He's even eaten a raw turtle egg once. "It tasted rank."

"LIVING" HIS BOOKS

Another book he's "lived" is *Dogsong*, his novel about an Eskimo boy's experience with dogsledding. "I've done 14,000 miles in the Arctic on dogsleds," says Gary.

"If I write about what sled dogs are like, it's because that's what happened. I've *done* these things."

Dogsong happened because Gary ran the Iditarod (a 700-mile dogsled race across the Arctic). During the race, he pulled into a village at about midnight. "A little nine- or ten-year-old kid comes running up and asks me to take my team to his house." Just then, Gary's dogs started to fight with each other. "I couldn't stop them," he recalls. "Anything in the middle of them gets ripped to pieces." Gary was terrified that the child was going to get hurt, so he picked him up over his head. "I don't think he weighed more than forty pounds." When Gary asked the child what he was doing, the boy responded, "I want you to teach me about dogs." At that moment, Gary realized he was looking at "an Eskimo kid finding his heritage."

When he talks with kids, Gary is very frank. "I tell them about the stupid things I did in my past." If one of the kids asks, "How come you did this?" Gary answers, "I screwed up." He explains, "I try not to sugarcoat things and say, 'It's okay if I do something wrong.' It's *not* okay. I try to be as honest as I can be. It really changes their attitude."

Gary works in four-day stretches, twelve hours at a time. Then he takes two days off. He estimates that he has written between 80 and 100 books. "A few years ago I found out that I have heart disease," he says. "It's not terminal, but it's not good, either. I'm on my endgame now. I know I will die, but I don't know when that will be. I decided that I would focus on work for the rest of my life."

Gary doesn't think of himself as being terribly important because he's a writer. "I don't elevate writers," he says. "I'm not a special person, or even slightly special. I think of myself as a chronicler. I think in feelings, emotions, and the sweep of life. Writer James Michener says the joy of writing is the loop and swirl of words on the page. It's a dance."

To those who like to write, he advises, "Read. Read like a wolf eats. Read what they tell you to read, and read what they tell you not to read. The writing will come. The writing itself is only an extension of reading."

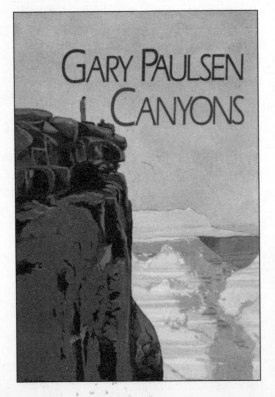

Even kids who don't like to write should be encouraged to read, Gary believes. "If you give them something they are interested in reading, they'll want to learn how it's put together. They'll wonder how the words work."

Gary Paulsen is always trying to learn more. "I realize I don't know very much, and I don't know how to write," he says. "I don't know how much time I've got left. If I don't watch it, I might blow my opportunity. I want to learn as much as I can about the rhythm and pace of life."

"If you want to learn about something, the Iditarod, running dogs, living in the bush, ripping up a town in Kansas, just go find out about it. Books can be part of what helps you find the answers to questions in your life."

DO IT YOURSELF!

Here is a writing activity from Gary Paulsen: "Write about things that are real and important. Get loose, have a good time. Write about your fantasies. Write about what's happening that you don't like—or that you do like."

Lynne Reid Banks

SELECTED TITLES

◆

Born:
July 31, 1929, in London, England

Home:
Dorset, England

If there's one question that Lynne Reid Banks dislikes being asked, it's: Where do you get your ideas? In her opinion, that's a lazy sort of question. "It seems to come naturally to people who don't think hard," she says. "If you think hard at all you realize that an author doesn't have a monopoly on ideas." Getting ideas isn't the hard part, in her opinion. "The trick is to catch them as they hurtle by like so many dust motes."

BREAKING ALL THE WRITING RULES

She'd rather be asked, "What's the toughest thing about writing a book?" The toughest part is seeing a good idea all the way through to a finished book, she believes. Another favorite question is, Are there any rules for being a writer?

There are hundreds of them, Lynne believes. "Lots of people make them and state them and write them in articles. Sometimes they call them tips. In my opinion, every one of them is made to be broken."

Lynne tends to visualize what she writes. "My whole aim and object in writing novels is to create a movie in the head of the reader," she says. "The readers must do some work with their own imagination, but the writer must make her own movie first. The two movies are never the same. That's why writing is so wonderful and why seeing a real movie based on a book you've enjoyed is always disappointing."

From time to time, Lynne gets stuck while she's writing. When that happens, she tries to sleep on it, to think about it at the very end of the evening. Sometimes the problem is solved when she wakes up. If it's not, then she might try talking out the writing problem. "It's very good if you've got somebody to listen to what you've done already, to see if you can see something in their reaction," she believes. Sometimes, when she reads works in progress aloud, new ideas will come to her.

But Lynne does not like to walk away from work that is incomplete. "When you're in the middle of writing something, you've got to stay close to it," she says. "If you allow yourself distance, you'll lose the thread of what you're trying to do. Writing every day is a good way to maintain your impetus. But it's not always possible."

The time to distance yourself from a manuscript is after the first draft is complete. "A few months ago, I finished a children's book," she said. "I thought this was magnificent, flawless, a masterpiece." She read it through several times. Then she went away for three

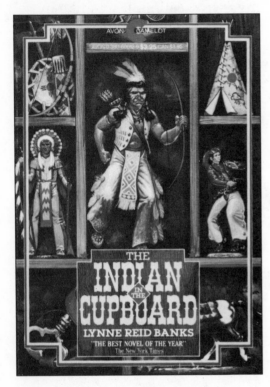

weeks. "I came back and read it again. The mistakes blared. They shot out and hit me in the face. I sat there in my freezing-cold workroom reading my 'masterpiece' and finding out it wasn't one."

As a child, Lynne enjoyed writing. But she didn't like to read. "It was only much later that I discovered that writing can only go to a certain point if you don't read," she says. "Your imagination becomes active when you read. And it's a scientific fact that your working vocabulary doesn't grow after you're about 11, unless you read."

To those who like to write, Lynne offers this advice: "Keep writing. There is no other thing to do. You've got to welcome each assignment, no matter how tough it is. Be grateful for the teacher who makes you exercise your imagination and writing skills. Join a drama club and act. Acting means getting into other people's skins, and creative writing requires the same activity."

Lynne Reid Banks also suggests that would-be writers keep journals. "But don't be boring and write things like *I had an egg for breakfast*," she advises. "You've got to emphasize the little things that make each day different from the last one. You've got to talk about feelings and reactions."

Journals should also include information about world events, says Lynne. "Don't be too self-centered or self-interested," she cautions. "It will be much more interesting later on to look back and realize that you noticed when there was an earthquake. It's never too soon to realize your corner of the world isn't all that matters."

DO IT YOURSELF!

Here is a writing activity from Lynne Reid Banks: "Take a situation in which a person like yourself receives bad news or is put in a very unusual position. For example, say you come home from school to find that everything has changed: your dog has died, your mother has gone to the hospital, your whole house has just disappeared, your parents have shrunk, and so on. Write about it."

"If you write without pictures in your head, you can't describe anything. You've got to have the play in your head the whole time, even if you're looking out from the eyes of your characters. If that fails, if that peters out, you're in trouble. You've got to get it going again."

Elizabeth George Speare

SELECTED TITLES

Calico Captive
1957

*The Witch
of Blackbird Pond*
(Newbery Medal)
1959

The Bronze Bow
(Newbery Medal)
1962

The Prospering
1967

The Sign of the Beaver
(Newbery Honor Book)
1983

◆

Born:
November 21, 1908, in Melrose, Massachusetts

Home:
Fairfield, Connecticut

Although Elizabeth George Speare can't remember a time in her life when she wasn't writing, it was not until she was in her forties that she began to write seriously. She began her career as a schoolteacher during the Depression. She married and then raised a family. When all of her children were in school, she began to write.

A HAUNTING CHARACTER

At first, she wrote about things she knew best: her home and her family. She sold those stories to magazines. "Then one day I stumbled on a true story from New England history with a character who seemed to me an ideal heroine," says Mrs. Speare. "For a long time, this girl haunted my imagination, and finally I began to write down her adventures, filling in the outlines of the actual events with new characters and scenes of my own creation. It was like living a double life, stepping every day from my busy world into another time and place and into a family that came to seem as familiar as my own."

That novel, *Calico Captive*, was published a few years later. And Elizabeth George Speare had found the type of writing that most absorbed her. She soon began work on a novel about a girl who moves from Barbados to the grim Puritan town of Wethersfield, Connecticut, in 1685. Before long, *The Witch of Blackbird Pond* was written.

"Almost all of the historical stories came from some incident that I read about in history that

sparked my imagination," says Mrs. Speare. "An idea settles in my mind, and when I'm ready, I write it."

Sometimes, an idea will settle there for a long time. The idea for her most recent book, *The Sign of the Beaver*, lay in the back of her mind for twenty years before she finally wrote it down. "I get letters from classes begging me to write a sequel to *The Sign of the Beaver*," she says. "The children can't bear the thought that the two boys might never see each other again."

As she writes, she does a great deal of research. As the story progresses, she keeps a pad of paper next to her. "Questions come up like, How long would it take to get from one place to another? or, What kind of transportation would they take? or, What does something cost?" she explains. Mrs. Speare writes down each question, looks up the answer, and inserts it in the story.

Mrs. Speare uses "an old, standard typewriter." She patiently rewrote each of her books three times, from beginning to end. "I write very slowly. I don't dash them off at all. Four or five pages a day is my limit," she says.

She sees pictures in her mind when she writes. As a scene forms, it begins as a still picture. But then it comes to life, and she feels she really has a story. "I not only see in pictures, but I feel as though I were there in the picture. I can feel as though I'm right in the room with the characters."

Writer's block occurs from time to time, but Mrs. Speare is very patient. "I wait. I wait until a good idea comes along. I've never felt any pressure to do otherwise," she says. Sometimes she reaches a point where she can't see how to

"In my school days I was never very fond of history. But I have discovered now that when I follow the adventures of an imaginary family through some great events of the past, the pages of the history books come alive for me."

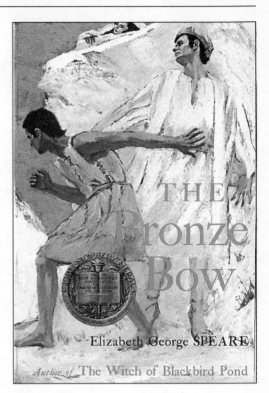

get to the next event. "I know where to go, but I don't know how to get there. At that point, I have to stop."

In her spare time, Speare loves to travel, to bird-watch, and to read. Her favorite books are biographies, autobiographies, and mysteries. "I like reading Ellis Peters. She's my favorite mystery writer. She writes about twelfth-century England. The books are full of wonderful history and wonderful details." In describing Ellis Peters's work, Mrs. Speare could be describing her own writing as well.

DO IT YOURSELF!

Here is a writing activity from Elizabeth George Speare: "Follow my own process. Take some little incident that you read about in a history book. Try to imagine that you are actually there while the incident is taking place. What would conversations around you be about? What would the place look like? What would it smell like?" Let your imagination take you to that place and time. Then write about it.

Mildred D. Taylor

SELECTED TITLES

Song of the Trees
1975

Roll of Thunder, Hear My Cry
(Newbery Medal)
1976

Let the Circle Be Unbroken
1981

The Friendship
1987

The Gold Cadillac
1987

◆

Born:
September 13, 1943, in Jackson, Mississippi

Home:
Boulder, Colorado

Mildred Taylor's stories come from deep in her imagination, itself a fire stoked by coals laid more than a century before by her African-American forebears. The stories passed on to Mildred by her father taught her, she has said, "a different history from the one I learned in school." She explains: "By the fireside in our Ohio home and in Mississippi, where I was born and where my father's family had lived since the days of slavery, I had heard about our past. It was not an organized history, beginning in a certain year, but one told through the years of slavery and beyond." Mildred's ancestors were ordinary people, who had done nothing more, she says, "than survive in a society designed for their destruction."

Her father's storytelling ability was magical to her. She yearned for a some of his talent. "I began to imagine myself as a storyteller, making people laugh at their own foibles or nod their heads with pride about some stunning feat of heroism," she recalls. Since she was shy and quiet, though, she did not feel comfortable talking before a crowd. "So I turned to creating stories for myself instead, carving elaborate daydreams in my mind."

The path to becoming a Newbery-winning writer was not at all direct. She went to college, worked for a time in the Peace Corps in Africa, and later attended journalism school at the University of Colorado. There, she became very involved in the Black Student Alliance, a group dedicated to increasing the school's commitment to teaching about the African-American experience.

HERITAGE AND PRIDE

Mildred has always felt that the sense of pride that many African-Americans feel for their families and their heritage is not communicated through traditional teaching materials. In elementary and high school, "there was no pride like that I felt when I heard the stories told by my father and other members of the family," she explains. "I remember once trying to explain those stories in class, about the way things really were. But the words didn't come out right—no one believed me. Most of the students thought I was mak-

MILDRED D. TAYLOR
Roll of Thunder, Hear My Cry

ing the stories up. Some even laughed at me. I couldn't explain things to them. Even the teacher seemed not to believe me. They all believed what was in the history books."

This ridicule only strengthened Mildred's determination to become a writer, to tell the stories as they really happened, and to be believed. But writing did not come easily to her. "Many times what I considered my best work was not good enough," she recalls. She did have one great success in high school while writing a story in the first person about an incident that had taken place in her family. "Without realizing it, I was telling the story in much the same language as when it was told to me. I was using the language of the family storytellers."

It took her a long time to understand that the language of the storytellers was her true writing voice. "Having read only fiction by white writers, I wanted to write like them, like the great

Do It Yourself!

Mildred Taylor first distinguished herself by writing down a real-life story that her father used to tell her. Think about the rich and interesting real-life stories that family members and friends have told you. Create a character and write one of those stories down in the form of a first-person narrative. Feel free to alter the facts to make the story stronger.

writers we had studied in class—Hemingway, Dickens, Austen, and the like." For many years she tried to emulate a literary form that, she says, "left my work sounding stiff and unconvincing. I could write well enough, but I could not convey what I wanted to convey with this style."

Years later, she discovered her voice. She had decided to enter a contest sponsored by the Council on Interracial Books for Children. She learned about the contest only a few days before the deadline, so she looked through several manuscripts she had already written to see if one would do. She pulled out a story based on one her father had told about trees being cut down on the family land during the Depression. She had tried writing the story from a boy's point of view and had failed. She had also tried writing from a grandmother's point of view and failed again. Both times, she had used the third person.

"I'm not sure where she came from," marvels Mildred Taylor years later, "but suddenly she was there: Cassie Logan, the story-teller. She emerged that propitious weekend with a fighting spirit, a great curiosity, and an unyielding pride. The storytelling tradition had always been in the first person. It was my heritage and I went with it." Mildred wrote the story all that long weekend. Without much sleep, she managed to finish the story in time for the deadline.

Several months later, she received a telegram announcing that she had won the contest. The book, which became *Song of the Trees*, was published and was well received. Her career as a writer had begun.

E. B. White

SELECTED TITLES

Stuart Little
1945

Charlotte's Web
(Newbery Honor Book)
1952

The Trumpet of the Swan
1970

◆

Born:
July 11, 1899, in Mount Vernon,
New York

Died:
October 1, 1985

In the 1920s, Elwyn Brooks White—or E. B. White as he is known to his many fans— took a train trip from New York City to the Shenandoah Valley in Virginia. "I got out, walked up and down in the Shenandoah Valley in the beautiful springtime, then returned to New York by rail," he wrote many years later. "While asleep in an upper berth, I dreamed of a small character who had the features of a mouse, was nicely dressed, courageous, and questing." When he woke up, he made a few notes about the mouse-child.

TALES OF A MOUSE-CHILD

When he had his dream, White (or Andy, as he was known by his family and friends) had never written a children's book. For most of his career, he had worked as a writer on the staff of *The New Yorker* magazine. But this little mouse had captured his imagination. So he began to tell stories about the mouse to his eighteen nephews and nieces. "I named him Stuart and wrote a couple of episodes about his life." White kept these stories in a desk drawer "and would pull them out and read them on demand." As years went by, he added more and more adventures.

"I learned two things from the experience of writing *Stuart Little*," White commented once. "That a writer's own nose is his best guide, and that children can sail easily over the fence that separates reality from make-believe. They go over it like little springboks."

White's other very well-known children's book reflects his years living on a farm in Maine. "A farm is a peculiar problem for a man who likes animals, because the fate of most livestock is that they are murdered by their benefactors. The creatures may live serenely, but they end violently, and the odor of doom hangs about them always." White kept several pigs, starting them in the spring as weanlings and feeding them all through the summer and fall. "The relationship bothered me. Day by day I became better acquainted with my pigs, and them with me, and the fact that the whole adventure pointed toward an eventual piece of double dealing on my part lent an eerie quality to the thing. I do not like to betray a person or a creature. It used to be clear to me, slopping a pig, that as far as the pig was concerned, I could not be counted on, and this, as I say, troubled me."

White started thinking of ways to save a pig's life. At the same time, he had been watching a big, gray spider at work. "I was impressed by how clever she was at weaving. Gradually, I worked the spider into the story—a story of friendship and salvation on a farm." Three years after he started writing it, *Charlotte's Web* was published.

His third children's book, *The Trumpet of the Swan*, was written many years later. This book was very hard for him to write. Of it, he wrote in a letter to a friend: "I am greatly handicapped by being unfamiliar with some of the terrain the story unhappily takes me into. I think it was extremely inconsiderate of my characters to lead me, an old man, into unfamiliar territory."

Charlotte's Web, among other books, was written in a small boathouse. White felt that in this spartan setting, he became a "wilder" and "healthier" man.

When he wrote children's books, he had very specific pictures in mind. Charlotte, he felt, should look exactly like a real spider. "When Garth Williams, the book's illustrator, tried to dream up a spider that had human characteristics, the results were awful." Finally, Charlotte ended up looking as White intended her to. "This natural Charlotte was accepted at face value," he said.

As a child, White was a brooder. "I was uneasy about practically everything," he said. He was the

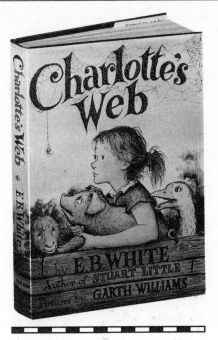

"All that I hope to say in books is that I love the world. I guess you can find that in there, if you dig around."

youngest in a large family, so he was usually in a crowd. But he often felt lonely and removed. "I took to writing early, to assuage my uneasiness and collect my thoughts, and I was a busy writer long before I went into long pants."

About writing, he once said, "I have always felt that the first duty of a writer was to ascend—to make flights, carrying others along if he could manage it. To do this takes courage, even a certain conceit."

E. B. White, who died in 1985, was unhappy about the state of the world toward the end of his life. But he felt that it was a writer's task to help others see the beauty of life. "Only hope can carry us aloft, can keep us afloat. Only hope, and a certain faith that the incredible structure that has been fashioned by this most strange and ingenious of all the mammals cannot end in ruin and disaster. This faith is a writer's faith, for writing itself is an act of faith, nothing else. And it must be the writer, above all others, who keeps it alive—choked with laughter or with pain."

DO IT YOURSELF!

Here is an writing activity based on the work of E. B. White: Read the description of a barn from Chapter Three in *Charlotte's Web* that begins: "*The barn was very large. It was very old. It smelled of hay and it smelled of manure. It smelled of the perspiration of tired horses and the wonderful sweet breath of patient cows. It often had a sort of peaceful smell . . . .*" Notice how E. B. White describes the barn: he describes how it looks, but mostly how it smells. Think of a place you know very well and like very much. Choose one sense: seeing, hearing, feeling, or smelling. Then use it to "explore" and write a description of that special place.

Celebrating Authors and Illustrators

SETTING UP AN AUTHOR/ILLUSTRATOR CENTER

Imagine you are visiting from a foreign land. In a matter of minutes, simply by glancing around, you can easily identify the kinds of things that are valued in the culture you are visiting.

For example: an outdoor sculpture suggests an appreciation of art; playing fields indicate a love for sports and fitness; statues of statespeople show a respect for leadership. The same can be said for our classrooms. Take a look around. What do we, as teachers, value? What messages, however subtle, are we sending to our "foreign visitors"—the students for whom these very rooms exist?

If we hang student writing or art on the walls, we are saying to children that we value their creativity. If shelves of children's books line our walls, we show our love for reading and literature. The classroom environment we create does much more than facilitate learning—it expresses our values, ideals, and ambitions for our students.

With this in mind, here are a few tips to help you set up author/illustrator centers:

- The most important thing is space. Allocate plenty of space for books, complete with cozy reading areas. This shows that reading is a valued activity.

- Set up a table upon which, each week or every couple of weeks, you highlight a particular author or illustrator. This table might include work by the author or illustrator, a photo, and letters to that person from students or the class.

- Encourage the class to write to publishers requesting information about favorite authors or illustrators. You may receive informational brochures, photos, bibliographies, or even newspaper clippings.

- Display student projects that tie into the creators' books. They can be drawings, related science projects, research papers, poems, stories, or whatever.

CELEBRATING BIRTHDAYS

As a nation, we celebrate the birthdays of Abraham Lincoln, George Washington, and Martin Luther King, Jr. Why not, as a classroom, celebrate E. B. White's or Molly Bang's? By celebrating a creator's birthday, we reflect on and commemorate his or her contribution to literature.

Here are a few tips for celebrating authors' and illustrators' birthdays in your classroom:

- For the week prior to the celebration, set up a table that displays the author's or illustrator's work and any biographical information you may have.

- On the big day, be sure to share plenty of the author's or illustrator's work with the class.

- Send the author or illustrator a birthday card. You might want to brainstorm together to think of an appropriate class gift for the author. Bruce Degen, the author and illustrator of *Jamberry,* might appreciate a jar of jam, for example.

- Ask students to bring in items related to the events, characters, or settings of the books. If your celebrated author is Robert McCloskey, for example, students could bring in drawings of mallard ducks, seashells, a harmonica, or even a bucket of blueberries for everyone to share.

- You or your students may want to dress up as characters from some of the books. Many teachers have been known to come in as Ms. Frizzle from Joanna Cole's *Magic School Bus* series. If the book is set in the past, dressing up can really be fun—and very educational.

- The important thing is to let your imagination run wild. Let the students actively contribute ideas. You might even want to serve birthday cake!

ADVENTURING WITH BOOKS

Books are wonderful springboards for all sorts of enjoyable learning activities—from putting on plays to serious class discussions, from creative writing to cooperative art projects. The important thing is to recognize the tremendous possibilities in good books. You've already captured student interest. Now you can build on that motivation by exploring further.

Here are some book-related activities you might want to try with the class:

Character Biographies

Invite students to write brief biographies of storybook characters. Encourage your students to make up details that weren't in the story but seem to fit the character. Illustrations are welcome too.

Story Patterns

A great way to help students appreciate the structure of stories is to recognize and imitate the patterns of their favorite books. With a little guidance, kids can do this with almost every book—from alphabet and counting books to more sophisticated folktales.

A Familiar Character in a New Situation

By reading, kids can "get to know" a character. You can put this knowledge to the test by asking students to put a familiar character in a totally new situation. Authors tell us that many stories are created by using this simple technique.

Writing Nonfiction

It's helpful for kids to realize that different types of books "do" different things. Science books, like Joanna Cole's *My Puppy Is Born*, give accurate information. Ask students to write a nonfiction book, such as *How to Care for Tropical Fish* if they have a household or class pet, or *How to Use the Library* or *A Day in the Life of Our Town*.

Interviews

The information about authors in this book is largely based on interviews. Students can interview each other, relatives, and community members. They first need to decide what they want to learn and make a list of questions. They may wish to capture the interview on an audio- or videotape recorder.

Joke and Riddle Books

Here's another form of writing kids can pursue. It may take some research, such as asking classmates and friends if they've heard any good jokes. They may want to team up with an artist who can illustrate the jokes. When creating this type of book, students become editors: they decide which jokes to include and where, and they help the illustrator come up with funny ideas.

Plays

When books feature lots of action and dialogue, they can easily be adapted to play form. Get students to write their own adaptations and then perform them. For the most fun, designate class members to be responsible for costumes, playbills, tickets—the works!

Illustrations

Some stories, such as classic folktales, lend themselves to many interpretations. Encourage students who exhibit an interest in art to respond to folktales by illustrating one. They should begin by writing out the text, without any pictures at all. Then they'll need to decide how many words go on each page. They may begin, like professional illustrators, by making rough sketches before the final versions. Other students can help out as editors.

For Homework . . . Forget Your Homework!

As you know, kids are often most creative when trying to explain why they didn't do their homework. You can turn this talent to advantage by giving the following assignment: "Today's homework is to make up a really good excuse for not doing your homework—the wilder the excuse, the better." You may want to gather and illustrate these stories in one collection: *Room 213's Book of Outrageous Excuses!*

What Happens Next?

Have students write sequels to beloved books. Kids understand this concept from movie sequels, so the assignment is the same: give us another story or adventure featuring the same character. They'll need to go back and look closely at the key elements of the first story, trying to incorporate similar elements into their new book.

NOTE: Remember, the primary purpose of literature is to give pleasure to the reader. Not every book or story necessarily has to be followed by a series of activities. Sometimes it's best to read a story aloud, close the cover, smile, and simply say, "Wasn't that wonderful!"

PHOTO CREDITS

Pg. 16: Alexa Brandenberg; pg. 20: courtesy of Putnam; pg. 24: Chuck Kelton; pg. 26: courtesy of HarperCollins; pg. 28: John Gilbert Fox; pg. 34: Laurence Hutchins; pg. 36: Bernie Goedhardt; pg. 38: Beverly Hall; pg. 42: Ian Anderson; pg. 44: Mary Velthoven; pg. 46: courtesy of Houghton-Mifflin; pg. 48: courtesy of Firefly Books; pg. 50: Myles Pinkney; pg. 56: Czeslaw Czaplinski; pg. 58: Joan C. Barker; pg. 62: courtesy of Houghton-Mifflin; pg. 64: courtesy of Houghton-Mifflin; pg. 80: Joan Potter; pg. 82: George Cooper; pg. 84: Edward Byars; pg. 86: Margaret Miller; pg. 90: Bob Newey; pg. 92: Helen Reynolds Studio; pg. 96: Susanne Singer; pg. 98: Jill Krementz; pg. 100: Garneau Studio; pg. 102: Tebby Stanley; pg. 108: Nancy Crampton; pg. 114: Jan Bindas; pg. 116: Judith Nulty; pg. 122: Jim Kalett; pg. 124: courtesy of Dutton; pg. 126: courtesy of Orchard Books; pg. 128: courtesy of Doubleday; pg. 130: Kathleen Kelly; pg. 132: Jack Ackerman; pg. 134: AP/Worldwide; pg. 143: Nicholas Sullivan, Skip Dickstein.

Authors' and Illustrators' Birthdays

Month/Day		Month/Day	
1/2	Jean Little	7/31	Lynne Reid Banks
1/28	Vera B. Williams	8/7	Betsy Byars
1/30	Lloyd Alexander	8/11	Joanna Cole
2/10	E. L. Konigsburg	8/12	Walter Dean Myers
2/11	Jane Yolen	8/18	Paula Danziger
2/12	Judy Blume	8/30	Donald Crews
3/2	Leo Dillon	9/3	Aliki Brandenberg
3/2	Dr. Seuss	9/4	Joan Aiken
3/3	Patricia MacLachlan	9/13	Roald Dahl
3/11	Ezra Jack Keats	9/13	Mildred D. Taylor
3/12	Virginia Hamilton	9/14	William H. Armstrong
3/13	Diane Dillon	9/14	John Steptoe
3/20	Mitsumasa Anno	9/15	Tomie dePaola
3/20	Lois Lowry	9/15	Robert McCloskey
3/21	Margaret Mahy	9/27	Bernard Waber
4/4	Phoebe Gilman	10/5	Louise Fitzhugh
4/8	Trina Schart Hyman	10/8	Barthe DeClements
4/12	Beverly Cleary	10/10	James Marshall
4/17	Martyn Godfrey	10/26	Steven Kellogg
5/9	Eleanor Estes	10/31	Katherine Paterson
5/17	Gary Paulsen	11/3	Monica Hughes
5/22	Arnold Lobel	11/14	William Steig
5/23	Scott O'Dell	11/16	Jean Fritz
6/10	Maurice Sendak	11/16	Barbara Reid
6/11	Robert Munsch	11/21	Elizabeth George Speare
6/14	Bruce Degen	11/28	Ed Young
6/18	Pat Hutchins	11/29	Madeleine L'Engle
6/18	Chris Van Allsburg	12/2	David Macaulay
6/25	Eric Carle	12/22	Jerry Pinkney
7/11	E. B. White	12/29	Molly Bang
7/13	Ashley Bryan		

Thanks to the librarians at Southworth Library, in Dartmouth, Massachusetts, James Preller, Kate Waters, and Terry Cooper. Thanks to Claudia Cohl and Dick Robinson for making so much possible. Thanks to Niko for his patience and to Sarah and Lucy for their inspiration.

D. K

Special thanks to Frank Hodge, Noriko Ichikawa, Deborah Kovacs, Angela Latal, Cynthia Maloney, Craig Walker, Caroline Webber, Phoebe Yeh, and especially Terry Cooper and Kate Waters. You all helped.

J. P.

We thank all the publishers who helped make this project possible as well as the many publicists, editors, agents, and personal assistants who helped us obtain information and direct access to the artists, especially Arnold Adoff, Amanda Allington-Baker, Virginia Amagnos, Peggy Butler, Amy Cohen, Anne Marie Davis, Colleen Donelson, Melanie Donovan, Julie Fallowfield, Peggy Guthart, Diane Kerner, Tony Lynch, Kim Magden, Elizabeth Miller, Iris Mills, Liv Irene Myre, Barbara Olsen, Jennifer Passamen, Sheila Quinn, David Reuther, Jennifer Roberts, Eleanor Rockman, Meghan Rowe, Charles Schlesinger, Tamar Schreibman, Paula Singer, Leonora Todaro, Sheila Watson, and Heather Zousmer.

Thanks to Lucy Evankow, chief librarian at Scholastic, and her staff of crack photo researchers, Donna Franklin, Rachel Gray, and Debra Thompson. Thanks to Jacqueline Swensen for her patience and a very special thanks to Liza Schafer for her dedication to this project.

We would also like to say a very special thanks to M. E. Kerr and Charlotte Zolotow for granting inteviews about their late friend and colleague Louise Fitzhugh.

Bibliography

Most of the material in this book was obtained through direct interviews with the authors and illustrators. In many cases, additional information was found in relevant books and articles.

The following books and book series were invaluable in our research: *Something About the Author* and *Something About the Author Autobiography Series*, both published by Gale Research of Ann Arbor, Michigan. Other helpful resources were: Lee Bennett Hopkins's *More Books by More People, Contemporary Authors,* and *Children's Literature Review.* (These resources are available in most libraries.)

GENERAL REFERENCE/ RESOURCE BOOKS

Bader, Barbara. *A History of American Picture Books: From Noah's Ark to the Beast Within.* Macmillan, 1976.
Contemporary Authors. Gale Research, 1962-.
Children's Literature Review. Gale Research, 1979-.
Field, Elinor W., and Bertha M. Miller,

eds. *Caldecott Medal Books: 1938-1957.* Horn Book, 1957.
Hoffman, Miriam, and Eva Samuels. *Authors and Illustrators of Children's Books.* Bowker, 1972.
Holtze, Sally Holmes. *Fifth Book of Junior Authors and Illustrators.* H. W. Wilson, 1983.
Hopkins, Lee Bennett. *Books Are by People.* Citation Press, 1969.
——. *More Books by More People.* Citation Press, 1974.
Kingman, Lee, et al. *Illustrators of Children's Books: 1956-1965.* Horn Book, 1968.
——. *Illustrators of Children's Books: 1967-1976.* Horn Book, 1978.
Kingman, Lee, ed. *Newbery and Caldecott Medal Books: 1956-1965.* Horn Book, 1965.
——. *Newbery and Caldecott Medal Books: 1966-1975.* Horn Book, 1975.
——. *Newbery and Caldecott Medal Books: 1976-1985.* Horn Book, 1986.
Kirkpatrick, D. L., ed. *Twentieth-Century Children's Writers.* St. Martin's, 1978.
Lacy, Lyn Ellen. *Art and Design in Children's Picture Books: An Analysis of Caldecott Award-Winning Illustrations.* American Library Association, 1986.
Lanes, Selma G. *Down the Rabbit Hole: Adventures and Misadventures in the Realm of Children's Literature,* 1971.
Once Upon a Time. Putnam, 1986.
Sendak, Maurice. *Caldecott & Co.* Farrar, Straus and Giroux, 1988.
Something About the Author. Gale Research, 1971-.
Something About the Author Autobiography Series. Gale Research, 1986-.

RESOURCE MATERIALS ON SPECIFIC AUTHORS
Mitsumasa Anno
Anno, Mitsumasa. "Why I Write and Paint." Transcription of speech as interpreted by Tadatoshi Akiba, n.d.
Aoki, Hisako. "A Conversation with Mitsumasa Anno." *Horn Book,* April 1983.
Marcus, Leonard S. "Travels with Anno." *Parenting,* October 1989.
Molly Bang
"Molly Bang." Biographical Material, Greenwillow Books, n.d.
Aliki Brandenberg
"Aliki." Biographical Material, Greenwillow Books, n.d.
"Aliki." Biographical Material, HarperCollins, n.d.
Brainard, Dulcy. "PW Interviews Aliki Brandenberg." *Publishers Weekly,* July 22, 1983.

Brandenberg, Aliki. "A Letter to the Class from Aliki." Trumpet Book Club, n.d.

Ashley Bryan

"Ashley Bryan." Biographical Material, Atheneum Publishers, n.d.

Bryan, Ashley. "On Poetry and Black American Poets." *Horn Book*, February 1979.

Marantz, Sylvia and Kenneth. "Interview with Ashley Bryan." *Horn Book*, March-April 1988.

Swinger, Alice K. "Profile: Ashley Bryan." *Language Arts*, March 1984.

Eric Carle

Carle, Eric. "Where Do Ideas Come From?" Transcription of speech given at the Library of Congress, n.d.

"Eric Carle." Biographical Material, Putnam, n.d.

"Face-to-Face with Eric Carle." *The Follett Forum*, n.d.

Laski, Audrey. "Painting with Papers." *London Times*, August 28, 1987.

"Meet the Author: Eric Carle." Scholastic Book Club, n.d.

Joanna Cole

"Doubleday Presents Joanna Cole." Biographical Material, Doubleday. n.d.

"Joanna Cole." Biographical Material, Morrow Junior Books, n.d.

"Joanna Cole & Bruce Degen." A Scholastic Author Tape, Scholastic, 1990.

"Scholastic Salutes Joanna Cole and Bruce Degen." Scholastic Book Club, n.d.

Donald Crews

"Donald Crews." Biographical Material, Greenwillow Books, n.d.

"Scholastic Salutes Donald Crews." Scholastic Book Club, n.d.

Roald Dahl

Dahl, Roald. *The Wonderful Story of Henry Sugar and Six Others.* Bantam, 1979.

Tomie dePaola

"An Interview with Tomie dePaola." *School Library Media Activities Monthly*, June 1976.

dePaola, Tomie. "Involved with Dreams." *Books for Your Children*, Summer 1980.

Raymond, Allen. "Tomie dePaola." *Early Years*, May 1983.

"Tomie dePaola." Biographical Materi-

al, Putnam, n.d.

Diane and Leo Dillon

Dillon, Diane. "Leo Dillon." *Horn Book*, August 1977.

Dillon, Leo. "Diane Dillon." *Horn Book*, August 1977.

——. "Leo and Diane Dillon." *Horn Book*, August 1977.

Dillon, Leo and Diane. "Caldecott Award Acceptance." *Horn Book,* August 1976.

——. "Caldecott Acceptance Speech." *Horn Book*, August 1977.

Phoebe Gilman

Gaitskell, Susan. "Phoebe Gilman." *Canscape Newsletter*, Spring 1986.

"Introducing Phoebe Gilman." The Canadian Children's Book Center, 1986.

Pat Hutchins

"Pat Hutchins." Biographical Material, Greenwillow Books, n.d.

Trina Schart Hyman

Hyman, Trina Schart. "Caldecott Medal Acceptance." *Horn Book*, July/August 1985.

——. *Self-Portrait: Trina Schart Hyman.* Addison-Wesley, 1981.

"Scholastic Salutes Trina Schart Hyman." Scholastic Book Club, n.d.

"Trina Schart Hyman." Biographical Material, Holiday House, n.d.

Ezra Jack Keats

"A Conversation with Ezra Jack Keats." Biographical Material, Macmillan, n.d.

"Ezra Jack Keats." Biographical Material, Macmillan, 1988.

Huston, Margo. "Honesty Is the Author's Policy for Children's Books." *Milwaukee Journal*, March 23, 1974.

Keats, Ezra Jack. "Caldecott Award Acceptance." *Horn Book*, August 1963.

——. "Collage." *Horn Book*, June 1964.

Lanes, Selma G. "Ezra Jack Keats: In Memoriam." *Horn Book*, September-October 1984.

Steven Kellogg

Kellogg, Steven. "A Letter to the Class from Steven Kellogg." Trumpet Book Club, n.d.

"Scholastic Salutes Steven Kellogg." Scholastic Book Club, n.d.

"Steven Kellogg." Biographical Material, Morrow Junior Books, n.d.

"Steven Kellogg . . . Teachers' Co-Conspirator." *Early Years*, January 1986.

"Steven Kellogg." The Trumpet Club Authors on Tape, Bantam, 1989.

Arnold Lobel

"Arnold Lobel." Biographical Material, Greenwillow Books, n.d.

"Arnold Lobel." Biographical Material, Harper & Row, n.d.

"Arnold Lobel: The Natural Illustrator, the Entertainer." *Early Years*, November 1980.

Hale, Robert D. "Musings." *Horn Book,* June 1987.

Lobel, Anita. "Arnold at Home." *Horn Book*, August 1981.

Lobel, Arnold. "Caldecott Medal Acceptance Speech." *Horn Book*, August 1981.

Marshall, James. "Arnold Lobel." Obituary. *Horn Book*, May-June, 1988.

Roback, Diane. "Arnold Lobel Remembered." *Publishers Weekly*, January 29, 1988.

David Macaulay

"David Macaulay." Biographical Material, Houghton Mifflin, n.d.

Robert McCloskey

Hale, Robert. "Musings." *Horn Book*, January/February 1989.

Meeker, Amy. "Boston Makes Way for Ducklings." *Publishers Weekly*, October 30, 1987.

"Robert McCloskey." Biographical Material, Viking Press, n.d.

James Marshall

"James Marshall." The Trumpet Club Authors on Tape, Bantam, 1989.

Marcus, Leonard. "James Marshall: An Ability to Convey Real Emotions in Ridiculous Situations." *Publishers Weekly*, July 28, 1989.

Robert Munsch

Davis, Patricia. "Kindergarten Superstar." *Report on Business Magazine*, December 1989.

"Introducing Robert Munsch." The Canadian Children's Book Centre, 1989.

Munsch, Robert. "Whatever You Make of It." *Canadian Children's Literature*, No. 43, 1986.

Mutton, Wayne. "The Story Teller: Robert Munsch." *Voyager*, Fall/Winter 1989.

Vanderhoff, Ann. "The Weird and

Wonderful Whimsy of Robert Munsch." *Quill & Quire*, May 1982.

Scott O'Dell

"Scott O'Dell." Biographical Material, Houghton Mifflin, n.d.

Jerry Pinkney

Davis, Andrea R. "Pinkney: Illustrating the Point." *American Vision*, April 1989.

Gaither, Edmund B., and Benjamin Peterson. "Interview with Jerry Pinkney." *Massachusetts College of Art*, 1987.

Meghn, Nick. "The Strength of Weakness: A Profile of Illustrator Jerry Pinkney." *American Artist*, January 1982.

"Scholastic Salutes Illustrator Jerry Pinkney." Scholastic Book Club, n.d.

Barbara Reid

Gaitskell, Susan. "An Interview with Barbara Reid." *Canadian Children's Literature* No. 56, 1989.

McDougall, Carol. "Barbara Reid." *Canscape Newsletter*, Spring 1988.

Maurice Sendak

Christopher, Rita. "A Child at Play." *Maclean's*, June 22, 1981.

Nuwer, Hank. "The Vision of Maurice Sendak." *Country Gentleman*, Winter 1981.

Sadler, Glenn Edward. "Maurice Sendak and Dr. Seuss: A Conversation." *Horn Book*, September/October 1989.

White, David E. "A Conversation with Maurice Sendak." *Horn Book*, April 1980.

Dr. Seuss

Bandler, Michael J. "Seuss on the Loose." *Parents*, September 1987.

Christy, Marian. "A Muse on the Loose." *The Boston Globe*, July 20, 1980.

Crichton, Jennifer. "Dr. Seuss Turns 80." *Publishers Weekly*, February 10, 1984.

Dowling, Claudia Gleen. "Dr. Seuss." *Life*, July 1989.

Dummit, Chris. "Still the Cat in the Hat's Meow." *Dallas Morning News*, June 16, 1983.

Gorney, Cynthia. "Dr. Seuss." *The Washington Post*, May 21, 1979.

Johnson, Tim. "Dr. Seuss: Architect of Social Change." *Whole Earth Review*, Summer 1988.

Karlen, Neal. "Yooks and Zooks from Dr. Seuss." *Newsweek*, January 16, 1984.

Sheff, David. "Seuss on Wry." *Parenting*, February 1987.

Wilder, Rob. "Catching Up with Dr. Seuss." *Parents*, June 1979.

William Steig

Allender, David. "William Steig at 80." *Publishers Weekly*, July 24, 1987.

Hearn, Michael Patrick. "Drawing Out William Steig." *Washington Post Book World*, May 11, 1980.

Kroll, Steven. "Steig: Nobody Is Grown-up." *The New York Times Book Review*, June 28, 1987.

Lanes, Selma G. "A Reformed Masochist Writes a Sunlit Children's Classic." *Harper's*, October 1972.

Steig, William. "Caldecott Award Acceptance." *Horn Book*, August 1970.

Van Gelder, Lawrence. "William Steig Shapes His Doodles into Prize-Winning Children's Books." *The New York Times*, November 18, 1977.

John Steptoe

"John Steptoe and Stevie." Biographical Material, Harper & Row, n.d.

"John Steptoe, 1950-1989." Obituary, *Publishers Weekly*, September 29, 1989.

Steptoe, John. "Mufaro's Beautiful Daughters." *Horn Book*, January-February 1988.

"Stevie: Realism Is a Book About Black Children." *Life*, August 29, 1969.

Watkins, Mel. "Stevie." *The New York Times Book Review*, October 5, 1969.

Mildred D. Taylor

"Mildred Taylor." Biographical Material, Viking/Penguin, n.d.

Chris Van Allsburg

Allis, Sam. "Rhinoceroses in the Living Room." *Time*, November 13, 1989.

Clemons, Walter. "Sailboats That Fly and a Train out of Nowhere." *Newsweek*, December 9, 1985.

Davis, William A. "Author Faces His Toughest Critic: Kids." *The Boston Globe*, November 6, 1990.

Macaulay, David. "Chris Van Allsburg." *Horn Book*, August 1982.

Van Allsburg, Chris. "Caldecott Medal Acceptance." *Horn Book*, August 1982.

———. "Caldecott Medal Acceptance." *Horn Book*, August 1986.

Bernard Waber

"Bernard Waber." Biographical Material, Houghton Mifflin, n.d.

"Bernard Waber." The Trumpet Club Authors on Tape, Bantam, 1989.

E. B. White

Elledge, Scott. *E. B. White: A Biography*. Norton, 1984.

Guth, Dorothy L., ed. *The Letters of E. B. White*. Harper & Row, 1989.

Vera B. Williams

"Vera B. Williams." Biographical Material, William Morrow, n.d.

Williams, Vera. "Boston Globe-Horn Book Acceptance." *Horn Book*, February 1984.

Jane Yolen

"Jane Yolen." Biographical Material, Crowell Junior Books, n.d.

"Jane Yolen." Biographical Material, Putnam, 1988.

Yolen, Jane. "Being Prepared for Serendipity." *The Writer*, May 1986.

———. "On Reading a Rejection Letter." *The Writer*, January 1981.

———. "The Once-a-Year File." *The Writer*, May 1984.

Ed Young

Brainard, Dulcy. "PW Interviews Ed Young." *Publishers Weekly*, February 24, 1989.

Edwards, Susan. "A Lot of Untalkable Things." *Vajradhatu Sun*, April-May 1982.

"Ed Young." Biographical Material, Putnam, n.d.

"Ed Young." Scholastic Book Club, n.d.

"An Interview with Ed Young." *Leader Notes*, January-February 1989.

DEBORAH KOVACS is the author of many books for children, including *A Day Underwater* (Scholastic, 1987) and *Brewster's Courage* (Simon & Schuster, Spring 1992). She lives in Massachusetts with her husband and two children.

JAMES PRELLER is the author of several books for children, including *How to Play Little League Baseball* (Kidsbooks, 1991) and *Kids Can Make a Difference* (Tor Books, Fall 1992). He lives with his wife, Maria, in Albany, New York.